# NAVIGATION AT SPEED

## A Motor Boat and Yachting Book

TIM BARTLETT

Fernhurst Books

This book first appeared as a six-part series in *Motor Boat and Yachting* magazine in 1991.

First published in book form in 1992 by Fernhurst Books, 33 Grand Parade, Brighton, East Sussex BN2 2QA

British Library Cataloguing in Publication Data
A catalogue record for this book is available from the British Library

ISBN 0 906754 76 3

## ACKNOWLEDGEMENTS

Our thanks to Imray, Laurie, Norie, and Wilson for permission to publish extracts from their Yachtsmen's charts, to Macmillan's for extracts from the Silk Cut Nautical Almanac, and to Thomas Reed Publications for extracts from Reed's Nautical Almanac and Coast Pilot (American East Coast Edition).

Photographs by Lester McCarthy, Bill Thomson, Alan Harper, Ralph Steele and Peter Cumberlidge.

Edited and designed by Joyce Chester.

Typeset by Central Southern Typesetters, Eastbourne
Printed by Ebenezer Baylis & Son, Worcester

Printed and bound in Great Britain

# CONTENTS

# 1

# DIVIDING UP THE WORLD

WHENEVER we move around, even on 'journeys' as simple and familiar as that between bedroom and bathroom, we are subconsciously navigating – estimating the direction and distance to 'landmarks' such as the corner of the dressing table, and using that information to work out where we are and where to go next.

But for longer journeys, or those in unfamiliar territory, such a casual approach to navigation isn't good enough, and memory has to be supplemented with a printed map.

## MAPS

Road maps show pictures of towns as though you were looking down on them from a great height. They are intended to accurately portray the distances and directions between the various features of the landscape. Distances have to be greatly reduced, of course. If dimensions are shrunk to 1/15840 of their actual size, then four inches on the map represents a mile on the ground. At this scale, many important features are too small to show up, so symbols are used instead.

As well as real objects, the map shows some completely imaginary features, in particular straight lines running from top to bottom and from side to side, which are all that can be seen of a grid system dividing the whole country into squares 1 kilometre across. This arbitrary pattern of squares means that the index in a book

of street plans can save you hunting all over the page by telling you that Elm Rise is in square D1, and allows a military commander to pinpoint a rendezvous in the middle of Dartmoor with a grid reference such as SX 636 678.

**Charts** – marine maps – are just the same as their dry-land counterparts, in that they are intended to be accurate representations of the earth's surface, reduced and flattened to fit onto conveniently-sized sheets of paper, and using symbols to represent important features.

One major difference is that instead of an arbitrary grid, positions on charts are defined by a natural, internationally-accepted reference known as **latitude and longitude.** This is important, because it is the key to our measurement of direction and distance.

## LATITUDE AND LONGITUDE

Our world is a slightly squashed ball spinning through space. Because it's spinning, we have two natural datum points – the ends of the 'axle', known as the **poles.** Midway between the poles is an imaginary line known as the **equator,** which serves as the baseline for the worldwide grid.

**Latitude,** according to the dictionary, is 'angular distance from the equator'. In other words, the latitude of a place is the angle measured at the centre of the earth between the place in question and the closest point on the equator (Fig 1).

If you were to draw a line round the globe linking all the places with a latitude of, say 50° North, it would be parallel to the equator – so it's called a **parallel.**

The other component of our natural grid system is known as **longitude.** There's no obvious baseline for

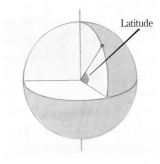

**1.** The latitude of any point on the earth's surface is defined as 'its angular distance from the equator'.

measurements of longitude: you could draw any number of lines from pole to pole, any one of which would do just as well as any other.

These lines are called **meridians** – and by common consent, one that passes through the Greenwich observatory (in London) is accepted as the 'Prime Meridian'. So (as Figure 2 shows), the longitude of a place is defined as 'the angular distance between its meridian and the Greenwich meridian'.

As both latitude and longitude are angular distances, they are measured in **degrees** – one degree being 1/360 of a full circle. But the Earth is so big that 1° of Latitude represents over 100 kilometres, or about 70 statute miles. This isn't precise enough for most practical purposes, so each degree is further subdivided into 60 **minutes.**

Traditionally, each minute was itself subdivided into 60 **seconds,** but although you may still come across seconds, they have fallen out of favour, and it's now more common to use decimal fractions of a minute – tenths, hundredths, or sometimes even thousandths.

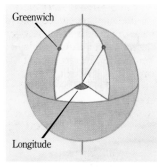

2. The longitude of a place is defined as 'the angular distance between its meridian and the Greenwich meridian'.

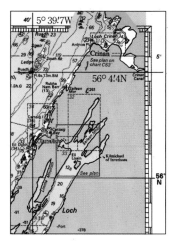

3. The latitude and longitude of Ryadh Sgeir, measured on the chart, is 56° 4'.4N 5° 39'.7W.

So the position of Ryadh Sgeir (near the entrance to the Crinan canal in western Scotland) is given as 56° 04'.4 North 005° 39'.7 West.

We can measure this accurately on the chart, helped by the meridians and parallels which run across it, and by the scales of latitude and longitude which form its borders – Latitude up each side, and Longitude across the top and bottom (Fig 3).

## DISTANCE

A minute of latitude is of particular significance, because it gives us the international unit of distance known as the **nautical mile.** Because the Earth isn't a perfect sphere, the actual size of a minute of latitude varies slightly, from 1843 metres (6046ft) at the poles to 1862 metres (6108ft) at the equator. The difference isn't really enough to worry about, but it's worth knowing that the standard nautical mile is taken to be 1853m (6078ft).

From the nautical mile comes the nautical measure of

speed: one nautical mile per hour is called a **knot.**

This intimate relationship between our measures of latitude and distance means that the latitude scales on the sides of the chart also serve as our scales of distance.

Measuring distance on the chart is easy, especially if you acquire a pair of **single-handed dividers** (Fig 4). They may look like something out of a museum, but the reason they haven't changed for centuries is because they are so very good at the job.

Measuring distance in the real world is more tricky – we'll be dealing with some of the ways of measuring out distance from landmarks later in the book. But it's even more important to be able to measure the distance we have travelled.

The instrument that does this is called a **log.**

Many small sports boats are fitted with a fairly simple log, which works by monitoring the pressure changes in a hollow tube sticking down into the water rushing past the hull. As the speed increases, so does the pressure in the tube – providing an indication of speed that is presented to the driver on a dial very much like a car's speedometer.

More sophisticated logs have a miniature paddle-wheel or impeller mounted under the hull, which turns as the water goes past. The log counts the number of turns, measuring the distance the boat has travelled (like a car's odometer) as well as its speed.

## DIRECTION

Imagine yourself in mid-ocean. There's nothing to distinguish one point on the horizon from any other. Without a point of reference, and no marked roads or tracks,

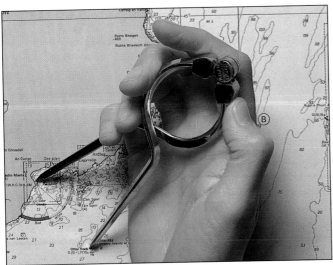

**4.** By holding single handed dividers like this, they can be opened or closed with one hand, to measure distances on the chart against the nearest part of the latitude scale. This leaves the other hand free to wield a pencil, or to brace yourself against the motion of the boat!

terms like left and right are almost useless.

But from the nautical navigator's point of view, there is a convenient reference, in the form of the invisible meridian that stretches away from him, around the globe, to the North and South poles.

The greatest navigational invention of all time was undoubtedly the **compass,** which made part of the meridian visible, and is still the most important of the navigator's tools.

In days gone by, directions were given names:
North – along the meridian towards the North pole
South – along the meridian towards the South pole
East – at right angles to the meridian towards the rising sun
West – at right angles to the meridian towards the setting sun.

These, and the intermediate terms North-east, South-east, South-west, North-west, and so on are still used for approximate directions even on land, but for navigation at sea they are obsolete: we now measure direction as an angle, measured in degrees counting clockwise from North (Fig 5).

## THE COMPASS

Technology has advanced a bit over the last couple of thousand years. **Gyro compasses,** able to indicate the true line of the meridian perfectly, have become commonplace on ships. But for most small craft, their size and price make them so completely impractical that we still rely on **magnetic compasses** based on those used by the Chinese over a thousand years ago. These work by sensing the Earth's magnetic field – which fortunately lines up quite well with the Earth's axis.

There are several types of magnetic compass.

A **steering compass,** as the name suggests, is used to guide the boat. In its usual form, it consists of a circular 'card', floating in alcohol in a transparent bowl. Magnets attached to the bottom of the card keep it lined up so that the 0/360 mark on the card points towards the **Magnetic North Pole** (Fig 6a).

A smaller, but essentially similar compass can be used to measure the direction between the navigator and a visible landmark. The direction of something from something else is called its **bearing,** so the hand-held instrument which measures it is called a **hand bearing compass** (Fig 6b).

A relatively recent innovation is the **flux gate compass,** in which the card and magnetic needles of the traditional compass are replaced by a ring of magnetic

**5.** Nowadays, directions are quoted in degrees, measured clockwise from North.

**6a.** A magnetic steering compass, well-placed in the driver's natural line of sight.

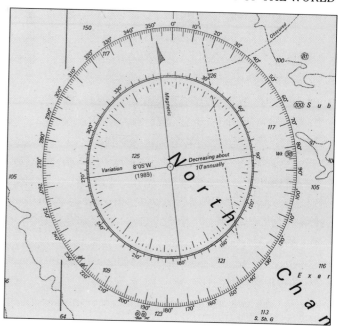

**7.** The outer ring of a chart's compass rose shows directions relative to True North: the inner rings show directions relative to Magnetic North.

**6b.** A hand bearing compass is used to measure the direction of landmarks.

sensors – flux gates – presenting their information on an electronic display or relaying it directly to an automatic pilot.

But whatever the virtues of a flux gate compass, it suffers the same fundamental drawback as any other magnetic compass: it doesn't actually show you where north is. Instead, it indicates the direction of the magnetic field it happens to be in at the time.

**Variation** is the name given to the discrepancy between the direction of the earth's magnetic field and its axis. Think of it, if you like, as being caused by the compass pointing towards a 'Magnetic North Pole' somewhere off the north coast of Canada, and

over 800 miles from the real pole. Just to add to the confusion, the Magnetic North Pole isn't fixed – it wanders about a bit, so Variation really does vary slightly from year to year.

It also varies from place to place. In the central Mediterranean and southern Sweden, for instance, Variation is negligible, but it increases to 10° off the west coast of Ireland. Similarly, in

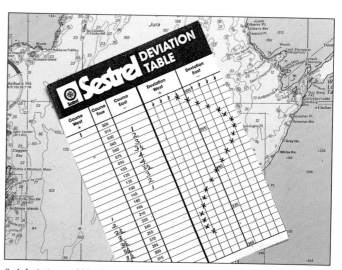

**8.** A deviation card like this will be provided by a compass adjuster to show the effects of the boat's own magnetic field on its steering compass.

## CHART SYMBOLS

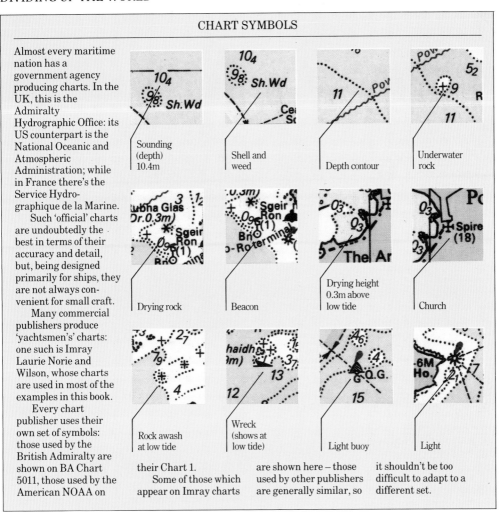

Almost every maritime nation has a government agency producing charts. In the UK, this is the Admiralty Hydrographic Office: its US counterpart is the National Oceanic and Atmospheric Administration; while in France there's the Service Hydrographique de la Marine.

Such 'official' charts are undoubtedly the best in terms of their accuracy and detail, but, being designed primarily for ships, they are not always convenient for small craft.

Many commercial publishers produce 'yachtsmen's' charts: one such is Imray Laurie Norie and Wilson, whose charts are used in most of the examples in this book.

Every chart publisher uses their own set of symbols: those used by the British Admiralty are shown on BA Chart 5011, those used by the American NOAA on

Sounding (depth) 10.4m

Shell and weed

Depth contour

Underwater rock

Drying rock

Beacon

Drying height 0.3m above low tide

Church

Rock awash at low tide

Wreck (shows at low tide)

Light buoy

Light

their Chart 1.

Some of those which appear on Imray charts are shown here – those used by other publishers are generally similar, so it shouldn't be too difficult to adapt to a different set.

the United States, it's negligible in the Florida Keys, but is almost 16° off the coast of Massachusetts.

Fortunately, it's very easy to find out the variation in your area – it's one of the many pieces of information shown on every navigational chart (Fig 7).

The other error to which magnetic compasses are prone is called **deviation.** It's the diffference between Magnetic North (shown on the chart) and Compass North (shown by the compass), and is caused by magnetic objects within the boat distorting the Earth's

magnetic field. Obviously the most significant deviations are caused by strong magnets, such as those found in loudspeakers and some electronic equipment, but electrical wiring or even tinned stores can have a significant effect.

The effect of all these influences varies, depending on the direction in which the boat is pointing, but a skilled compass adjuster can usually reduce the error to within a few degrees. He will then draw up a **deviation card,** showing the remaining deviation (Fig 8).

Once you know about an error, you're 90% of the way towards overcoming it. In the case of variation and deviation, the treatment is summed up in a single word: CADET – an acronym for **C**ompass **Add E**ast **T**rue – and what it means is that to get from a compass bearing to a true one, you should add easterly errors.

So if your compass reads 150°, and the Deviation card shows an error of 5° East, your course is:

      150° (Compass)
$+$    5° E
$=$  155° (Magnetic)

But if the Variation (shown on the chart) is 10° East:

155° (Magnetic)
+    10° E
=  165° (True)

You don't have to be a mathematical genius to work out that to convert the other way, from True to Compass, you'll have to subtract Easterly errors.

Westerly errors are exactly the reverse.

So if your compass reads 345° and the Deviation is 3°W your course is 342° (Magnetic) and if the Variation is 8°W your course is 334° (True)

All three numbers, 345° (C), 342° (M), and 334° (T) refer to exactly the same direction, but it's as well to get used to the idea of translating from one 'language' to the other.

Like 'boot' in German and 'boot' in English, 345° (C) and 345° (T) mean completely different things!

Hand bearing compasses, by the way, are never corrected for deviation, nor do they have deviation cards. There would be no point: because they are portable, they can be used anywhere on the boat, with different deviating influences in each location. Rather than risk applying the wrong deviation, it's safer to assume that the deviation on a hand bearing compass is 0°.

## DIRECTION ON THE CHART

Although there's only one really practical way to measure distance on the chart – dividers – there's quite a wide choice of instruments for measuring direction, each of which has advantages for particular purposes.

Charts are printed with several **compass roses** (Fig 7), each showing True directions on the outer ring,

**9.** Using parallel rulers to transfer directions to and from a compass rose. Line up one ruler with the required direction, and press down firmly while moving the other ruler away. Then press down on the second ruler while you move the first up to it.

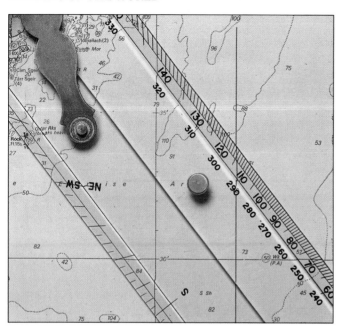

**10.** Captain Field's markings save a lot of 'walking'. Place the rulers (closed) on the chart so that a convenient meridian cuts the required direction on the scale of degrees and simultaneously touches the tip of the S mark.

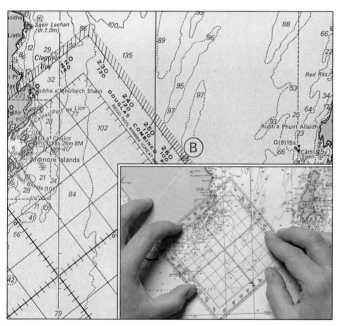

**11.** If the Douglas Protractor is placed on the chart so that the central hole is on a meridian, and the same meridian passes through the required direction on the inner scale, the edges of the protractor will indicate the bearing.

and Magnetic directions in an inner ring. On some charts, an even smaller, fainter circle shows Magnetic directions again, but using the old-fashioned 'points' notation.

The classic instrument for transferring directions from the compass rose to other parts of the chart is a set of **parallel rulers.** This consists of a pair of rulers, joined together with hinged arms so that once one ruler has been lined up on the nearest compass rose, the rulers stay parallel while they are 'walked' across the chart (Fig 9).

With practice, this is quick, easy, and foolproof, but it requires a big, reasonably steady chart table – not something often found in fast motorboats!

A variation, known as **Captain Field's pattern** parallel rulers overcomes this problem by having its own compass rose built in (Fig 10). These are excellent at the planning stage of a passage, and so long as the chart table is big enough, can be used equally effectively under way.

For very small or lively boats, a better bet is one of several types of protractor – of which the air navigators' **Douglas Protractor** (Fig 11) is probably the most widely used.

IMAGINE, for a moment, that you're in St Peter Port, in the Channel Islands. Out beyond the harbour entrance are the nearby islands of Herm, Jethou, and – a few miles further away – Sark.

Even a glance at the chart (Fig 1) is enough to tell you that the total distance from St Peter Port to one of the anchorages on the far side of Sark is no more than about 10 miles (Fig 2). A more careful look shows that although you could head straight from St Peter Port to L'Etac (a big rock just off the tip of Sark), that would mean going through a narrow, rocky passage south of Jethou. A safer route would be from the harbour entrance to the Lower Heads Buoy, then across to L'Etac.

Your intended route can be drawn onto the chart as a series of straight lines using parallel rulers or a Douglas

# 2

# WITH THE
# FLOW

protractor, and a soft pencil – preferably a 2B, which can be rubbed out easily later.

Because you'll be steering with a magnetic compass, it makes sense to translate the True directions of these lines (read from the chart) into Magnetic at this stage, by

applying the variation shown on the compass rose.

The length of each leg can be measured, too, by using a pair of dividers and the scale of nautical miles provided by the latitude scales on the sides of the chart.

So the first leg of this passage is:

a distance of 2.4 miles in a direction of 130° (T) which corresponds to 135° (M)

Having planned your route, loaded the picnic box, and topped up the fuel and water tanks, you set off. Clearing the pier, you alter course to 135° (M), and open the throttle to a comfortable cruising speed of 22 knots.

Five minutes later, one of your crew asks where you are.

Using a Speed-Time-Distance calculator or mental arithmetic, it's easy enough to work out that in five minutes at 22 knots you have covered

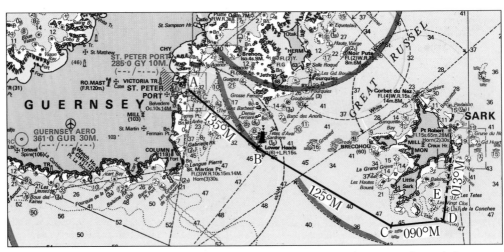

**1.** From St Peter Port, the planned route leads south of Lower Heads buoy and L'Etac, then turns north towards the anchorage. The wavy line symbols indicate overfalls. A, B, C, D and E are waypoints: see panel on page 17.

**2.** Dixcart Bay, on Sark's east coast, is just ten miles from St Peter Port.

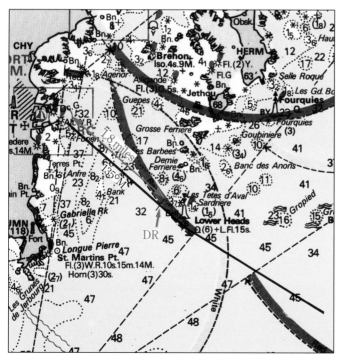

**3.** A DR (dead reckoning) is based on course and distance only.

$(5 \div 60) \times 22 = 1.8$ miles.

Having steered in the direction of your pencil line on the chart, and covered 1.8 miles from the pier head, it seems logical to assume that a mark on the pencil line, 1.8 miles from the pier head would represent your position (Fig 3).

In a way, it does. It's called a **DR**, or **dead reckoning** position. 'Dead', in this case means 'deduced', because you've deduced it from your course and distance. But although dead reckonings certainly have their uses, they very rarely show where you really are.

In our example, the DR suggests that the Lower Heads buoy should be half a mile away, and almost directly ahead. In practice, you'd probably find it some way off to one side.

## WIND

Sailors develop 'wind sense' almost automatically. They have to: without it, their boats don't go. In a motor boat, the wind is less obvious. It might make the sea rough, but once under way our own speed masks its subtleties.

Slow down, though, and its effect becomes obvious, blowing the boat downwind so that her movement through the water is at an angle to her course.

This angle is called **leeway** – and it's impossible to measure accurately. If you're lucky enough to have smooth water in spite of a strong wind, you might get some idea of the boat's real movement through the water by looking at the direction of her wake. But in the windy conditions in which leeway is most significant, this is seldom possible, and you have to rely on experience.

Leeway always pushes the boat downwind of her course and generally increases when:

- the wind is at right angles to the course
- the wind is strong
- the sea is rough
- the boat speed is low
- a hood or canopy is up
- there's a human helmsman rather than an autopilot (because humans tend to err downwind)

Leeway can amount to 15° or more, but in most reasonable conditions it's unlikely to exceed about 5°. In any case, unless you know your boat well enough to be confident of your estimate, it's usually better to ignore leeway rather than risk using a grossly over-estimated figure.

### TIDE

We can be much more positive about the effects of the tide.

In the UK, the necessary information is provided in two forms: either as **tidal diamonds** (Fig 4), or as **tidal stream atlases** (Fig 5).

But using any of them demands some understanding of the tides themselves. We'll be looking at tides in more detail – and at the slightly different way tidal stream predictions are presented in the USA – in Chapters 4 and 5, but for the moment it's enough to appreciate that they are caused by the gravitational force of the moon pulling on the world's oceans, making the sea level rise and fall in a complicated but predictable rhythm.

**Tide tables,** giving those predictions, are available from many different sources (Fig 6), but whoever publishes them, they take much the same form (Fig 7).

The times and heights of tide vary from place to place, so the tide tables are divided into sections, each giving the predictions for a particular **standard port.**

They show the times of high and low water for each day of the year, with a note at the top of the page pointing out the time zone in use. Alongside each time is a height, showing the predicted height of the water above a standard level known as **Chart datum.**

On May 1, for example, Low water at St Helier is at 0204 GMT, with a height of 1.6m, and rises to 10.3m at High water at 0745. The difference between high and low water is called the range of the tide – in this case 8.7 metres.

But a week later, on the 7th, High water is 7.7m and

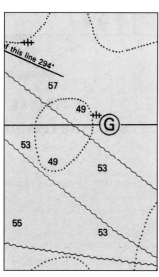

**4.** A tidal diamond – so called because on Admiralty charts they are diamond shaped – refers to a table of tidal stream data elsewhere on the chart. The symbol close to the north west represents a wreck.

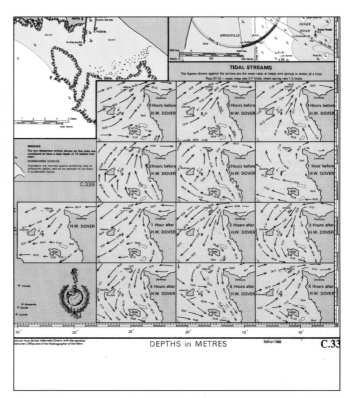

**5.** Tidal atlases like this one from the Imray chart show the tidal streams pictorially.

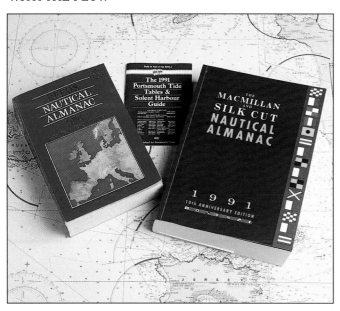

**6.** Apart from official government publications, tide tables are included in yachtsmen's almanacs and in wallet-sized booklets.

**7.** St Helier tide tables for the first week of May 1991. Tide tables show the times and heights of high and low water at standard ports for every day of the year.

the following low water is 4.2m – a range of just 3.5 metres.

This weekly alternation is caused by the sun, whose gravity sometimes helps the moon to produce a bigger than average tide, called a **spring;** and sometimes hinders it, producing a smaller than average tide called a **neap.**

Of course, the huge quantity of water required to raise the sea level around St Helier by 8.7 metres (almost 30 feet) has to come from somewhere. It's all this water moving from place to place that we see as **tidal streams.**

Tidal stream atlases are published as separate books, in yachtsmen's almanacs, and on some charts. They are made up of thirteen chartlets, each of which shows the tidal streams at a particular moment. Figure 8, for example, shows the tidal streams around the Channel Islands 4 hours before High Water at Dover.

It doesn't matter that

Dover is 200 miles away: High Water Dover is merely a convenient reference to relate the complex cycle of the tides to clock times. We can look up the tide tables for Dover to find that on May 1, High Water Dover will be at 1321 BST (1221 GMT). So the chartlet is showing us what the tidal streams are doing at 0921 (four hours before High Water Dover on that day). Others show the situation at 1021, 1121, and so on.

The directions of the tidal streams are indicated by the arrows, with their rate – how strong they are – shown by the numbers. Between Guernsey and Sark, for instance, the chartlet shows a rate of 20,36.

This isn't really one rate, but two: 20 represents the rate of the tidal stream during Neap tides, 36 its rate during Springs. Both are in tenths of a knot.

If we were midway between springs and neaps, we could estimate that the rate will be midway between 2.0 knots and

3.6 knots, or 2.8.

Tidal Diamonds – so called because on a British Admiralty chart they are marked by magenta diamonds – are dotted around the chart. Each one refers to a table of tidal streams printed somewhere on the same chart.

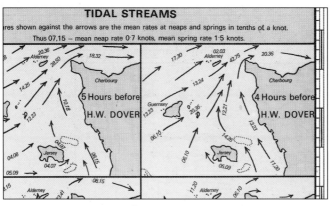

**8.** Each chartlet of the tidal atlas shows the tidal streams at a particular moment in the tidal cycle.

---

## THE RIGHT TRACK

There are so many lines involved in traditional chartwork that it's easy to be confused by what they all represent. Even if you don't use them all in high speed navigation, it's useful to distinguish between different kinds of direction on the chart.

**Ground track** – often just called **'track'**, refers to the boat's movement over the land and can be shown on charts as:

**Wake course** – sometimes called the **'water track'**, refers to the boat's movement through the water and can be shown on charts as:

**Course** – refers to the direction the boat is being steered and can be shown as:

## 095°M

**Heading** – refers to the direction in which the boat is pointing at any moment and is not necessarily the same as its course.

**Set** – The direction in which the tidal stream is flowing and can be shown on charts as:

**Bearing** – the direction of one object from another.

---

| 49°29·0' N 2°02·5' W | | ST. HELIER | | | | | | | ST. HELIER | | | | | |
|---|---|---|---|---|---|---|---|---|---|---|---|---|---|---|
|  |  | 6 | 5 | 4 | 3 | 2 | 1 | HW | 1 | 2 | 3 | 4 | 5 | 6 |
| Direction |  | 197° | 186° | 174° | 153° | 102° | 029° | 015° | 004° | 351° | 345° | 327° | 204° | 196° |
| Rate in | Springs | 2·3 | 2·1 | 1·7 | 1·2 | 0·7 | 1·4 | 2·0 | 2·3 | 2·2 | 1·5 | 0·5 | 1·3 | 2·1 |
| Knots | Neaps | 0·9 | 0·9 | 0·7 | 0·5 | 0·3 | 0·6 | 0·8 | 0·9 | 0·9 | 0·6 | 0·2 | 0·6 | 0·9 |
| Position 49°20·0' N 2°22·2' W | | Hours before H.W. at ST. HELIER | | | | | | | Hours after H.W. at ST. HELIER | | | | | |
|  |  | 6 | 5 | 4 | 3 | 2 | 1 | HW | 1 | 2 | 3 | 4 | 5 | 6 |
| Direction |  | 239° | 232° | 205° | 133° | 068° | 063° | 055° | 045° | 035° | 004° | 282° | 242° | 237° |
| Rate in | Springs | 3·1 | 2·6 | 1·4 | 0·8 | 1·5 | 2·2 | 2·3 | 2·0 | 1·4 | 0·7 | 0·7 | 1·8 | 3·0 |

**9.** The tidal stream tables on charts show the set and rate of the tidal stream at each of the tidal diamonds.

---

Figure 9 shows part of just such a table. Like the tidal stream atlas, the information is referred to the time of High Water at a standard port – in this case, it happens to be St Helier.

According to the tide tables, High water at St Helier on 1 May is at 0745 GMT or 0845 BST. So if we are interested in the tidal stream at 0945 BST, we look down the '1 hour after HW' column to find that the the tidal stream at 'G' is setting in a direction 004° and that as this is a Spring tide, its rate is 2.3 knots.

Tidal diamonds give more precise information than tidal atlases, but it's more difficult to assimilate. And because even 'G', the diamond closest to our route, is 5 miles away, it isn't really very relevant.

For most small boat navigation, tidal atlases are very much more useful.

### ALLOWING FOR WIND AND TIDE

Equipped with the necessary information, it's now relatively easy to improve on the DR by adjusting it to account for the wind and tide.

Take the wind first. If we estimate our leeway to be about 5°, caused by a wind blowing from the south, our movement through the water is not 135° (M), as the compass says, but 130° (M).

So after we've travelled 1.8 miles through the water, our amended DR is shown in Figure 10.

Now for the tidal stream, which is flowing north eastward at 3.6 knots.

In the 5 minutes it has taken us to move 1.8 miles through the water, the water itself must have moved (5 ÷ 60) × 3.6 = 0.3 miles north-eastward.

That's allowed for by

## WAYPOINTS

Some points along the route are of particular navigational significance. These are called waypoints.

On our passage from Guernsey to Sark, there are five waypoints:
A – St Peter Port harbour entrance
B – close south of Lower Heads buoy
C – south of Sark
D – south-east of Sark
E – east of Sark

Most electronic navigation aids require numbered waypoints, but there's no reason why you shouldn't give them letters or names.

It's convenient if a waypoint is easily identifiable when you reach it – like our waypoint B – but it's important to remember that the route dictates the location of the waypoints, not vice versa.

In our example, it would have been tempting to pick a waypoint just off L'Etac instead of points C and D. But had we tried this, the route would have led very close to the shallows south of Sark and right over the rocks called Les Vingt Clos.

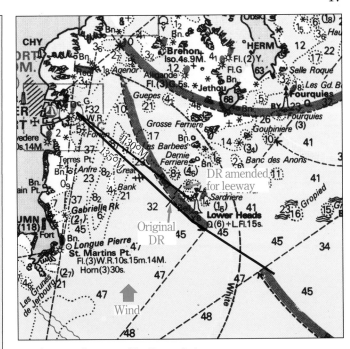

**10.** The DR can be improved by allowing for leeway.

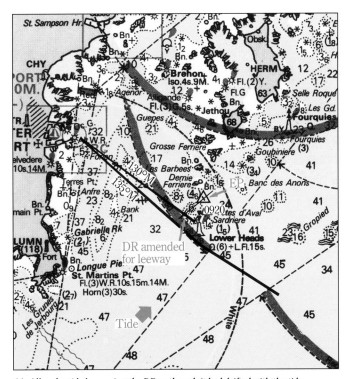

**11.** Allow for tide by moving the DR as though it had drifted with the tide.

moving the amended DR north eastward 0.3 miles (Fig 11).

The end result is the best possible estimate of our real position, so it's called, logically enough, an **EP** – for **estimated position.** An EP is conventionally indicated by a triangle and should always be labelled with the time.

### WISE BEFORE THE EVENT

In this example the EP not only shows why the buoy isn't directly ahead, but also that if

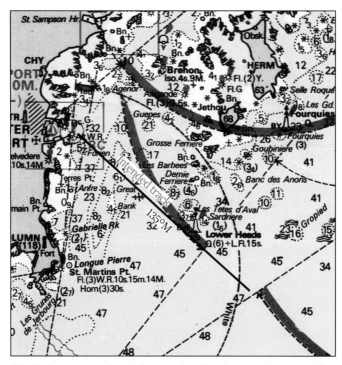

**12a.** To shape a course, draw in the planned track, and estimate the time it will take to cover that distance.

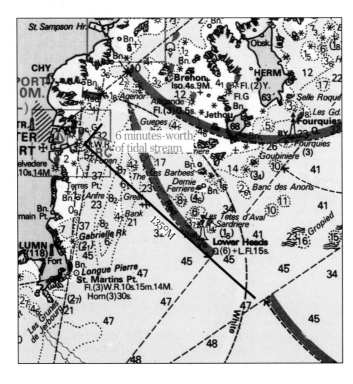

we'd been doing this for real, we'd have just had a lucky escape – by the time we'd fiddled about with the chart and tide tables to work it out, we'd have slipped through the rocks more by luck than judgement.

It's much more useful to be able to allow for the wind and tide in advance, so that instead of steering down our planned line, and then wondering where we've got to, we can 'aim off' just enough to make the pencil line represent our movement over the ground.

This is called **shaping a course,** and the traditional way of doing it is almost exactly the reverse of plotting an EP.

Start by drawing in the line along which you intend to travel – the intended track (Fig 12).

Guess how long you're likely to take to cover that leg of the passage, and round it off to some figure which will make the subsequent arithmetic easy. One hour is most convenient, but six minutes is almost as good, because it's exactly one tenth of an hour. Besides, it's a very much more realistic estimate for this short leg.

Draw a line – the tide vector – from your starting point to represent the effect of the tide over your chosen period of time: 6 min at 3.6 knots = .36 miles north east.

With the dividers set to the distance you expect to cover in the same time (6 minutes at 22 knots = 2.2 miles) and one point of the dividers on the end of the tide vector, use the other point to make a mark on the intended track.

**12b.** From the starting point, draw a line representing the effect of the tide in that time.

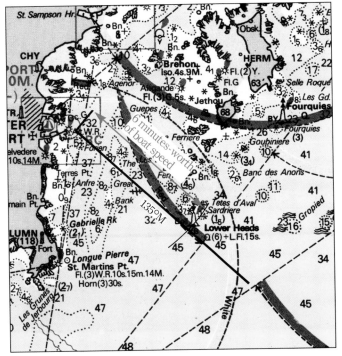

**12c.** Set the dividers to the distan... the boat should travel through th... water in that time, and with one poin... on the end of the tide vector, mark across the required track with the other.

A line drawn between the two points of the dividers now represents the course you need to make through the water.

If you expect to make leeway, you need to allow for this separately to arrive at a course to steer. The rule is easy to remember if you think of an old admiral TAKING PORT with his dinner to prevent wind: TAKE leeway off if the wind is on the PORT side.

## SPEEDING IT UP

All this chartwork works well enough on a sailing boat or a slow motor cruiser where there's time to spare, but on a fast-moving boat it may well take longer to work out a course to steer than you'll spend steering it! Even more to the point, it requires so much fiddly chartwork that it's often impossible once you're under way.

The alternative is to use the **'One in Sixty Rule'**.

Essentially this says that if you steer one degree off course for sixty miles, you'll end up one mile off course.

Similarly, if you steer ten degrees off course for sixty miles, you'll end up ten miles off course.

And if you steer ten degrees off course for six miles you'll end up one mile off course.

Looked at the other way, if you want to counter a tide which will push you one mile off course on a six-mile leg, you should steer 10° up-tide.

The rule can be summed up as: $\dfrac{\text{Tidal stream rate} \times 60}{\text{Boat speed}}$

= Course adjustment

**12d.** The line from the end of the tide vector to the mark across the track indicates the course to steer.

In practice, you'd have to be a mathematical whizz-kid to work this out quickly and accurately, because

[3.6 × 60 ÷ 22 = 9.8]

isn't exactly the easiest of sums.

But you can usually round the figures off:

3½ × 60 ÷ 20 ≏ 10

. . . not spot-on, but near enough for practical purposes.

The 1 in 60 rule gives the correction for tidal streams setting across your intended track. Those at an angle of about 45° warrant about half the 1 in 60 correction, while those directly ahead or astern won't push you sideways, so you don't need to allow for them at all.

There's just one proviso: the 1 in 60 rule can't be relied on if the tide is so strong – or your boat so slow – that the correction amounts to more than 30°.

## QUESTION

The day after our trip to Sark, you intend leaving St Peter Port to go to St Helier.

Your first waypoint is 20 miles away, and your intended track is 152° True.

You expect to cruise at 22 knots, making 3° leeway due to a southerly wind (i.e. blowing from the south), and in a tide flowing north east at 2 knots.

What is your compass course, allowing for variation of 5° West and deviation of 2° East?

## ANSWER

| | |
|---|---|
| Intended track | 152° (T) |
| Correction for tide | +5½° |
| Correction for leeway | +3° |
| Course to steer | 160½° (T) |
| Variation 5°W | +5° |
| | = 165½° (M) |
| Deviation 2°E | −2° |
| Course to steer = 163½° (C) | |

IT'S one thing to put a triangle on the chart to represent an EP (estimated position): quite another to pin your faith on it.

Even if boats really travelled at constant speeds and in straight lines, logs are rarely completely accurate; compasses and helmsmen are prone to errors; the forecast tidal streams are only approximations; and the allowance for leeway is never more than an educated guess.

So an EP isn't really a position, so much as the middle of an ever-expanding 'pool of errors'. And although practice and experience will help keep the size of the pool to a minimum – and help you judge it's likely size – they won't stop it growing.

You can, however, make a fresh start with a new and smaller pool – as shown in Chapter 2 by aiming to pass very close to a buoy. Going close to any identifiable charted feature immediately tells us where we are, and reduces the pool of errors to a few yards.

## GETTING YOUR BEARINGS

So let's suppose we've hopped from buoy to buoy along the Solent, and are now heading along the coast to Weymouth, forty miles away. Just south of Poole the chart shows a prominent headland, where the tide sluicing over an uneven seabed causes a patch of rough water extending more than four miles offshore. It's over fifteen miles from the last buoy, so your pool of errors could easily be a mile across,

# 3

# GETTING A FIX

but you'll need to be pretty sure of your position to avoid the overfalls.

The solution is neatly summed up by the expression **'getting your bearings'**.

If the hand bearing compass shows that the lighthouse on Anvil Point is 335° (Magnetic) from us, we must be somewhere on a line drawn in a 335° (M) direction that passes through the lighthouse (Fig 1a).

We can do the same thing with Handfast Point, which in this case is on a bearing of 015° (M). And as there's only one place which can be on both these **position lines** at once, that must be where we are (Fig 1b).

Or is it? What if we misread the compass? Or if the compass itself were a few degrees out? Or if we'd mistaken Peveril Point for Handfast Point?

A third bearing, of St Alban's Head, will resolve the issue, crossing with the other two to form what is called a **three-point fix** (Fig 1c).

The fix is completed by putting an arrowhead on one end of each line (to show that it's a bearing), drawing a circle round the position (to show that it's a **fix**), and labelling it with the time at which it was taken.

It would be very reassuring if the fix consisted of three

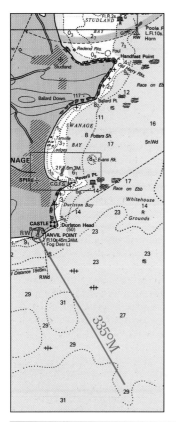

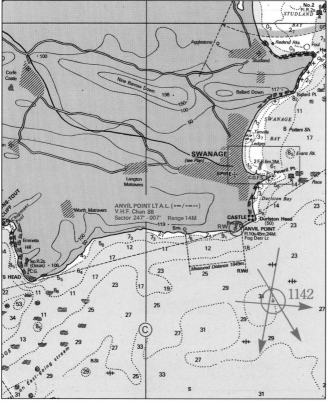

**1.** Taking a three-point fix. If the hand bearing compass shows that Anvil Point lighthouse is 335° (M) from us, we must be on a line drawn in a 335° (M) direction that passes through the lighthouse. By taking bearings of Handfast Point and St Alban's Head and drawing similar lines on the chart, we know that we are within – or just outside – a 'cocked hat' bordered by these three lines.

lines crossing at a single point, but in practice they almost invariably form a triangle, called a **cocked hat.** We could be anywhere inside the triangle – or even just outside it – but it's usual to assume that you're at its centre – keeping in mind that the bigger the cocked hat, the less reliable the fix.

In a fast-moving boat several factors conspire to prevent you getting a neat, accurate-looking fix. By far the most significant is the boat's movement: in the time between the first and last bearings, a 20-knot boat may well have moved half a mile. So it's important to take bearings as quickly as possible, especially those at close range or almost directly abeam, which will be changing quickly.

Your choice of landmarks can make a difference too. If we'd misread the bearing of Handfast Point by 5°, it would have thrown the fix out by about 4 **cables** (0.4 miles) (Fig 2a).

But if we'd chosen to use Durlston Head instead, and had made exactly the same mistake, the fix would have been almost 8 cables adrift. In trendy navspeak born of the electronic age, this is called GDOP – **geometric dilution of precision** – but in everyday language you'd say it's because the angle between the two bearings is small (Fig 2b).

So what happens if we'd used the Needles, still just about visible some fifteen miles astern? The bearing is 073° (M), so the position line cuts that of Anvil Point at a very healthy 98°. But it's so far away that five degrees of deviation produce a position error of 1¼ miles (Fig 2c).

There are four simple rules to help produce good fixes:
● Choose landmarks that can be positively identified and are clearly marked on the chart.
● Choose near landmarks rather than distant ones.
● Choose landmarks which will produce position lines which cut at a large angle – ideally about 60° if you have three landmarks, 90° if you have two.

● Aim for an accuracy of about 5° – but take short-range bearings quickly, and long-range bearings carefully.

## SPEEDING IT UP

A major snag with this kind of fix is that it is very difficult to use a hand-bearing compass on a lively, bouncing boat. Flux gate compasses are easier to use than swinging-card types, and you could always slow down – but that's not a very satisfying approach to high speed navigation.

One alternative is to use the boat's steering compass. It's much less prone to violent swings, and you don't have to hold onto it. All you have to do is aim the boat at your chosen

landmark for a few seconds, and note the compass heading (Fig 3a). It's not quite so easy, but you can use a similar technique to take bearings of objects astern (Fig 3b).

This technique can even be adapted to take the bearing of an object well off to one side, by sighting across a bulkhead or the back of a seat to judge when it's directly abeam. Adding or subtracting 90° to the heading shown by the steering compass at that moment will give you the bearing (Fig 3c).

But plotting the bearings once you've got them can still be something of a problem, so it's a good idea to look around for ways to reduce the amount of chartwork involved.

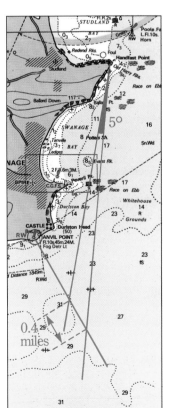

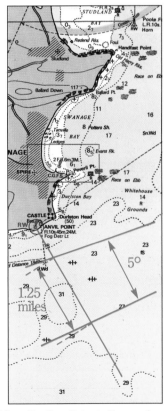

2. Taking bearings at speed. Errors can be reduced by choosing nearby landmarks with position lines that cut at large angles. If we'd misread the bearing of Handfast Point by 5°, for example, it would have thrown the fix out by 0.4 miles. But the same bearing error on Durlston Head or the distant Needles would have increased this to 0.8 miles or 1.25 miles respectively.

**3.** Using the steering compass to take bearings of landmarks ahead, astern, and abeam.

One method is to plan the route so that, if possible, there is a suitable landmark directly on the intended track. That way, if everything is going according to plan, the pencilled line showing your intended track will serve as one of your position lines. And if your second position line is taken from something directly abeam, you probably won't need to do any plotting at all – it's so easy to judge a right angle that the abeam bearing can often be drawn in by eye. If not, you can always use a corner of the Douglas Protractor.

On our trip from the Solent to Weymouth, for instance, the first leg might well head straight towards Anvil Point. The helmsman will appreciate this, because it gives him something to aim at, and he'll probably steer more accurately as a result. And so long as the headland is dead ahead whenever the compass

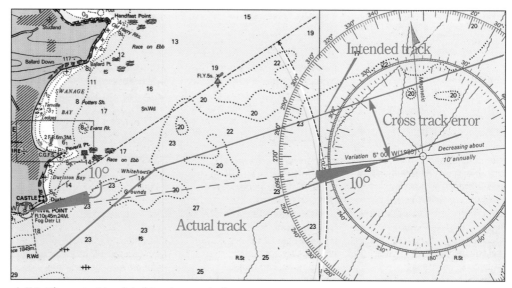

**4.** Using the one-in-sixty rule to determine cross-track error.

reading corresponds with our intended track, we know we're on track.

If it's not, there's still a way to put a position line on the chart without a lot of drawing, by using the 1 in 60 rule that we looked at in Chapter 2.

This says that if you steer one degree off course for sixty miles, you'll end up one mile off course; if you steer ten degrees off course for sixty miles, you'll end up ten miles off course; and if you steer ten degrees off course for six miles you'll end up one mile off course.

Suppose, half way across Poole Bay, we notice that instead of Anvil Point being dead ahead on 257° (M), it's more like 267° (M). If the land seems to be further north than it should be, we must be too far south. And as it's 10° off track at a range of about six miles, the one in sixty rule says that we must be about a mile off track – or, in navspeak, that we have a **cross-track error (XTE)** of one mile (Fig 4).

## READY-MADE POSITION LINES

The best possible position line would be one that requires no measuring, no instruments, and no chart work whatsoever. And there are plenty of them around.

They're called **transits.** The textbook definition of a transit is 'two or more objects on the same bearing from an observer' – a rather convoluted way of saying that a transit is two objects which appear to be in line with each other.

Heading west towards Anvil Point, we should be able to see Durlston Head, the white cliffs of Handfast Point, and the coastline dropping away towards Poole.

But when we cross the invisible line – the transit – which passes through the tip of both headlands, Handfast Point will disappear behind Durlston Head. The line can be drawn on the chart in advance, assuring us of an instant, highly accurate position line (Fig 5).

The trouble with transits is that they don't crop up at your beck and call – you have to look for them in advance, and grab a position line whenever one presents itself. But the opportunity is too good to be missed.

## OTHER METHODS

The other snag with transits is that they very rarely occur in pairs – and while one position line on its own can be useful, it's never quite as good as two or three combining to make a fix.

We could, of course, take a bearing of St Alban's Head. But we could, almost as easily, look downwards, to the seabed. Most boats with any pretensions towards cruising have an **echo sounder,** giving a continuous indication of the depth of water. The rise and fall of the tide means that the depths (soundings) shown on the chart very seldom correspond to the actual depth of water, but we'll be dealing with this in Chapter 4: for the moment let's just assume that as we cross the Handfast/Durlston transit the echosounder reading (corrected for tide) shows that we're in an area where the sounding is 30 metres.

If the seabed were smooth and gently-sloping, that wouldn't be much help, but here, where there are pronounced changes in depth, the 30m contour itself is a perfectly reasonable position line. It's somewhat ambiguous, because it wriggles around so much that it cuts the transit at three different points, but at least it

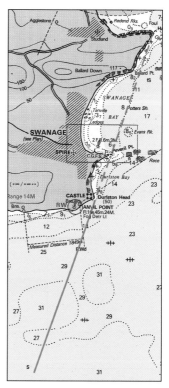

**5.** Transits. Heading west towards Anvil Point, we should see Durlston Head, the white cliffs of Handfast Point, and the coastline dropping away towards Poole. But as we cross the invisible line which passes through the tip of both headlands, Handfast Point will disappear behind Durlston Head.

suggests that we can't be more than a hundred yards or so inshore of our intended track, or more than about ½ mile outside it (Fig 6).

One thing that would certainly sort out this uncertainty would be if we knew our distance offshore.

**Radar** would do the job easily – as described in another Fernhurst book by the same author, *A Small Boat Guide to Radar* – but for short distances it's possible to make a reasonable estimate of range without any sophisticated equipment whatsoever.

Yet again, it's an application of the 1 in 60 rule.

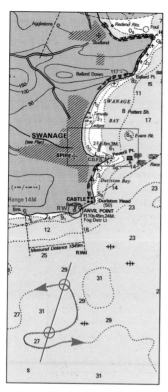

**6.** Using a 30m depth contour to find your approximate position.

or thicker fingers, it might be 1½°, while if your arms are longer or your fingers thinner you might be lucky enough to have a straightforward 1°.

The chart gives a brief description of Anvil Point lighthouse, telling us that it shows a flashing light (Fl) once every 10 seconds (10s), with a nominal range of 24 miles (24M), from a height of 45 metres (45m).

So if the top of the 45m (150ft) lighthouse appears to be almost a complete finger's width above the shoreline, we must be about 1½ miles away from it (Fig 8).

## MOVING POSITION LINES AROUND

Although we've been thinking mostly in terms of fixes, there aren't really that many occasions in a fast boat when you really need to know exactly where you are. You're far more likely to be concerned either with your cross track error or with the distance to the next waypoint than with both at once.

So one position line at a time is often enough – and there are plenty of potential sources of position lines:
- visual bearings
- transits
- soundings
- estimated ranges
- not to mention electronic aids.

But once in a while you'll find yourself desperate for a fix, but with only one position line available. A classic example is off the north coast of France, where two delightful rivers are guarded by over four miles of rocky ledges. It's forty miles from Guernsey, so your pool of

If you're looking at something 100 feet tall from a distance of a mile, it would appear to be 1° high – because 100 feet is almost exactly 1/60 of a mile. An object 200 feet tall one mile off would be 2° high, and at ½ mile would grow to 4°.

So long as you remember that 1° = 100ft at 1 mile, it's easy to work out the rest – or you can look it up from the tables published in almanacs such as *Reed's* and *Macmillan's* (Fig 7).

Although the tables are intended to be used with a sextant, for rough measurements at short ranges it's enough to know that one finger's width at arm's length is just over a degree. One of my ¾in wide fingers, for example, on the end of my 34in arms, is 1¼°. If you've got shorter arms

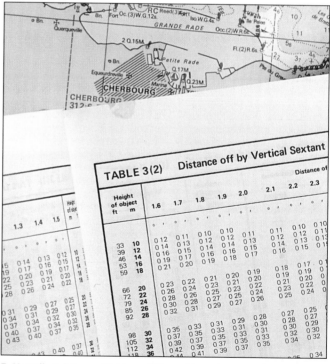

**7.** *Macmillan's* distance-off tables could be used in conjunction with a sextant to calculate how far away you are from an object of known height.

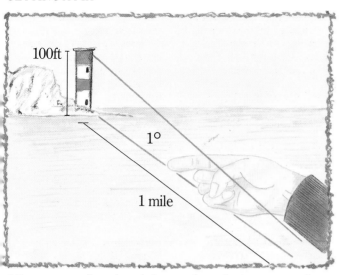

**8.** You can use your fingers instead of a sextant for rough measurements at short ranges. A finger's width at arm's length is just over one degree.

passes through the 'EP' (Fig 9b).

This is called a **transferred position line,** and, although it's bound to be less reliable than the original bearing, it can be used in just the same way, and crossed with another position line – such as another bearing of Roches Douvres – to produce a **running fix** (Fig 9c).

The chartwork involved doesn't make a running fix a particularly attractive proposition in a fast boat, but it's still worth keeping at the back of your mind. Besides, there's a variation which cuts the chartwork right down to size.

Suppose you'd noted the time and log reading when Roches Douvres was 45° off the bow, and again when it's directly abeam. You could use this information to plot a running fix, but in this case you don't have to: by picking the right moment, the geometry has been arranged so that the distance you've travelled over the ground is the same as your distance from the lighthouse (Fig 10).

errors could easily have grown so large that the first you'd know of a rock would be the bump!

The saving grace is a lighthouse called Roches Douvres. It too is surrounded by rocks, but it's easy enough to get a bearing (Fig 9a).

That one bearing doesn't produce a fix, but choosing an arbitrary spot on the position line would at least give a starting point from which to plot an EP. Over a fairly short distance the EP wouldn't be very far out – except, of course, that you didn't really start from your chosen position but from a line passing through it. So you must now be on another line, parallel to the first, which

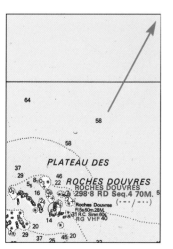
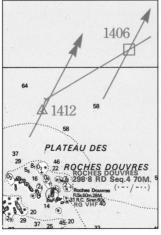
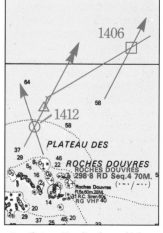

**9.** Transferred position lines. Take a bearing of a landmark, and choose an arbitrary spot on that position line from which to plot an EP. A few minutes later, you'll be on another line, parallel to the first and passing through the 'EP' – a 'transferred position line'. If you then take another bearing, you'll have two position lines, forming a running fix.

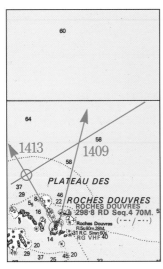

**10.** Note the time and log reading when Roches Douvres is 45° off the bow, and again when it's directly abeam, and the distance you've travelled over the ground will be the same as your distance from the lighthouse.

ELECTRONIC AIDS

Electronic navigation aids are really outside the scope of this book: like radar they are the subject of another Fernhurst publication: *A Small Boat Guide to Electronics Afloat.* But it's useful to have some idea of how the more popular systems work.

**Decca, Loran, Transit,** and **GPS** are all position fixing systems, using radio signals from transmitters on land or in satellites. On-board receivers process the signals to present a digital read-out of Latitude and Longitude.

Most are also capable of memorising a number of waypoints, and performing the relatively simple trigonometry required to translate the Lat and Long position into the range and bearing of the next waypoint, or into the cross-track error.

**Decca and Loran C**

Decca and Loran are ground-based systems, similar in principle but operating on different frequencies and covering different areas. Both use groups of transmitting stations (called **chains**), each consisting of a **'master'** station surrounded by up to four **'slaves'**. The slaves' transmissions are perfectly synchronised with those of their master, so if a slave's signal is received later than that of its master's, it must be further away.

So if the time difference (Loran) or phase difference (Decca) corresponds to a distance of, for example, 6 miles, the receiver must be somewhere on a position line on which every point is six miles further from the slave than from the master. Comparing the master signal with each of its slaves produces several position lines, which intersect just like visual bearings to form a fix.

Although both systems can be accurate to about 20 metres, their fixes are affected by GDOP, interference, atmospheric effects, and by the calculations involved in translating the fix into Lat and Long, so their accuracy is typically more like 100–200 metres, and at extreme range or at night can deteriorate to 3000 metres.

**Transit**

Transit is a satellite system, already more than 25 years old. It consists of five satellites in such low orbits that they have to whip round the earth at almost 15,000 knots.

Just as the sound of a car's engine seems to drop in pitch when it goes past, the frequency of the radio signal received from a fast-moving satellite drops abruptly as it passes, so the receiver knows when the satellite reaches its

closest point of approach. As the satellite's signal also includes details of its position and movement, that's enough for the receiver's computer to calculate a position line. On the same principle, it can calculate other position lines for as long as it can hear the satellite – gathering enough information in 10–15 minutes to produce a fix.

Unfortunately, the boat's own movement complicates things. Every ½ knot of error in boat speed causes a position error of about 200 metres and takes the overall accuracy of the system out to about 500 metres.

**GPS**

The other drawback of Transit is that fixes can only be achieved when a satellite happens to be passing – and satellite passes may be as much as two hours apart.

This is being overcome with the **Global Positioning System (GPS),** which will eventually use 21 satellites in such high orbits that a receiver anywhere in the world should be able to listen to four of them at a time.

The heart of a GPS receiver is a clock, synchronized with the clocks in the satellites, so that the time taken for each satellite's signal to reach the receiver can be measured. Radio waves travel at a constant speed, so the time interval relates directly to the distance between the satellite and the receiver, to give a position line.

Radio waves travel so fast (almost 600 million knots) that if the receiver's clock were even a millisecond slow the cocked hat would be over 150 miles across. But a GPS receiver automatically adjusts its clock so as to achieve the smallest possible cocked hat.

The potential accuracy of the Global Positioning System

## QUESTION

After spending a day in Weymouth, you're heading further west. You passed a yellow buoy off Portland harbour 10 minutes ago, and then altered course to 182° (M). You've been making 20 knots, so you should now be very close to the West Shambles buoy, but you can't see it.

Portland Bill is directly abeam, and there's another headland about 25° off your starboard quarter (bearing approximately 335° (M)). Where are you?

is better than 20 metres, but it's a military system, so the signals available to civilian users are deliberately degraded to induce random errors of about 100 metres.

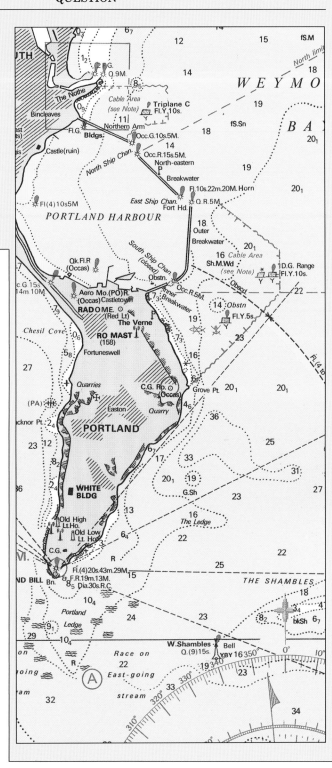

## ANSWER

It's fairly obvious (from the fact that Portland Bill is abeam) that we're not yet far enough South, while the rough bearing of the other headland (Grove Point) suggests that we're also too far East. This would probably be confirmed by the echo sounder showing a deeper reading than it should, but shoaling very quickly as we head towards the Shambles Bank. If you were really lost it would be worth slowing down or stopping to plot these two position bearings and a contour line as a fix. The problem shows what can happen if you rely too much on a wrongly-identified buoy: but it also shows the value of working out your ETA at the next waypoint!

IF you never plan to cruise anywhere but the Mediterranean or the Baltic, you might as well skip this chapter! But in most of the world's seas, tides are a fact of life, raising the water level in one place, lowering it in another, and setting up horizontal movements of water between the two.

As we saw in Chapter 2, these tidal streams can be strong enough to sweep even a fast-moving boat off course, towards the rocks we were trying to avoid.

But before condemning tides as an unmitigated nuisance, bear in mind that

# 4
# SPHERES
# OF
# INFLUENCE

the changing water level can fall low enough to reveal those rocks and turn them into useful landmarks, or rise high enough for us to float harmlessly over the top.

These changes of sea level don't happen purely by chance. They're governed by the movement of the earth and moon around the sun, so they are almost as predictable as sunrise and sunset. Even so, you'd have to be impossibly clever to predict all you might need to know about tides just by watching the skies.

High and low water

Fortunately, all the complicated work is done for us by national authorities such as the British Hydrographic Office, and the American National Oceanographic and Atmospheric Administration.

All we have to do is know how to use the information that's provided. And to do that, we need to understand the language of the tables!

## THE TIDAL CYCLE

Over most of the world the tides follow a fairly simple pattern, in which the sea level rises for just over six hours, then takes about the same length of time to fall. The result is an alternating pattern of high and low waters, with two of each in every 25 hours or so.

The difference in level between **low water** and **high water** is called the **range** of the tide.

Even in one place, the range of tide is never exactly the same from one day to the next: some tides have very low lows and very high highs, giving a big range. These are called **spring tides,** or **springs.** Others have relatively high low waters and low high waters, and are called **neaps** – but talk to a native Channel Islander and he'll pronounce the word as 'nip' – a good reminder that a neap tide is a small one!

It takes about a week for the tides to change from springs to neaps, and another week to change back – a half-monthly cycle superimposed on the half-daily pattern of highs and lows.

Finally, there's an even slower, half-yearly cycle. It's much less marked than the others, but still worth knowing about, because the half-yearly cycle means that a mid-summer or mid-winter spring tide will have a smaller range than one in spring or autumn.

## LEVELS AND DATUMS

When sea level keeps changing like this, it poses chart-makers with something of a problem. They need some constant level, known as **chart datum**, against which to measure depths and heights.

Most countries, including Britain, follow an international resolution which requires chart datum to be 'a level so low that the tide will not frequently fall below it' by setting their chart datums to correspond to the **lowest astronomical tide** (LAT).

As its name suggests, LAT is the lowest level to which the tide is expected to fall

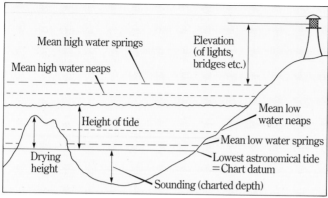

**1.** Chart datum on British charts is the lowest level to which the tide is expected to fall, based on astronomical predictions. Water levels and drying heights are all given with respect to chart datum, but the elevation of lights, bridges, etc. are all given with respect to mean high water springs.

In the USA, chart datum is **mean lower low water** (MLLW). The fact that these include the word 'mean' suggests that they are all based on some kind of average – so there are bound to be some low waters that are below chart datum. So you can't assume that there will always be as much water as the chart suggests.

That all sounds horribly complicated, but unless you plan to get involved with ocean passage making or charter a boat on another continent you needn't worry about it – just get used to your own country's chart datum and tide tables. In this chapter, we'll stick to the British system: Chapter 5 will deal with the American system.

according to astronomical predictions. This means that on British charts you can safely reckon on having at least as much water as the charted depth (Fig 1).

But beware: weather conditions can occasionally force the sea level below LAT.

Other countries have, for various reasons, adopted other chart datums: in non-tidal waters like the Baltic, it is often **mean sea level** (MSL), while Denmark uses **mean low water springs** (MLWS).

### TIDE TABLES

The tide tables show the height of the tide above chart datum (Fig 2).

So if we were going into Plymouth at 1316 GMT on 16 May, a glance at the tide tables is enough to show us that the water should be 0.8 metres above chart datum – give or take a bit to allow for weather conditions.

So in the buoyed passage between Drakes Island and the shore, where the chart (Fig 3a) shows a sounding of 2.1 metres, we'd expect to find 2.1 + 0.8 = 2.9 metres of water.

Just to the east, the chart shows a patch of rocks, the yellow tint indicating that they sometimes appear above water, and the **drying height** of 2.7 showing that they are 2.7 metres above chart datum.

But with 0.8 metres of water above chart datum, they will be only 2.7 − 0.8 = 1.9 metres above the surface (Fig 3b).

Try the same thing a few hours later, at 1933 GMT, and

### ENGLAND, SOUTH COAST - PLYMOUTH

TIME ZONE UT (GMT)
For Summer Time add ONE hour in non-shaded areas

LAT 50°22'N          LONG 4°11'W

TIMES AND HEIGHTS OF HIGH AND LOW WATERS

| | MAY | | | | | JUNE | | | | | JULY | | |
|---|---|---|---|---|---|---|---|---|---|---|---|---|---|---|
| | TIME | m | | TIME | m | | TIME | m | | TIME | m | | TIME | m |
| **1** W | 0054 0657 1309 1912 | 1.1 5.2 1.2 5.2 | **16** TH | 0056 0715 1316 1933 | 0.7 5.3 0.8 5.4 | **1** SA | 0140 0742 1353 1957 | 1.5 4.8 1.6 5.0 | **16** SU | 0217 0836 1435 2050 | 0.8 5.1 1.0 5.4 | **1** M | 0203 0808 1416 2020 | 1.3 4.9 1.4 5.1 | **16** TU |
| **2** TH | 0125 0724 1338 1939 | 1.3 5.0 1.4 5.1 | **17** F | 0140 0759 1400 2015 | 0.8 5.2 1.0 5.3 | **2** SU | 0214 0816 1428 2032 | 1.5 4.7 1.7 4.9 | **17** M | 0303 0922 1521 2135 | 1.0 5.0 1.2 5.2 | **2** TU | 0238 0840 1452 2052 | 1.3 4.8 1.5 5.0 | **17** W |
| **3** F | 0156 0751 1408 2009 | 1.5 4.8 1.6 4.9 | **18** SA | 0226 0845 1446 2101 | 1.0 5.0 1.2 5.1 | **3** M | 0251 0854 1506 2111 | 1.6 4.6 1.8 4.8 | **18** TU | 0351 1009 1609 2222 | 1.2 4.8 1.4 5.0 | **3** W | 0315 0915 1531 2127 | 1.4 4.7 1.6 4.9 | **18** TH |
| **4** SA | 0227 0824 1440 2045 | 1.6 4.7 1.8 4.8 | **19** SU | 0315 0935 1535 2151 | 1.2 4.8 1.5 5.0 | **4** TU | 0333 0938 1550 2157 | 1.7 4.5 1.9 4.7 | **19** W | 0441 1058 1701 2313 | 1.4 4.7 1.7 4.9 | **4** TH | 0356 0954 1614 2210 | 1.5 4.6 1.7 4.8 | **19** F |
| **5** SU | 0303 0906 1518 2131 | 1.8 4.5 2.0 4.6 | **20** M | 0408 1030 1630 2247 | 1.5 4.6 1.7 4.8 | **5** W | 0421 1030 1642 2251 | 1.8 4.5 2.0 4.7 | **20** TH | 0535 1151 1758 | 1.7 4.6 1.9 | **5** F | 0442 1044 1704 2304 | 1.6 4.6 1.9 4.7 | **20** SA |
| **6** M | 0347 1000 1606 | 2.0 4.3 2.2 | **21** TU | 0508 1131 1733 | 1.7 4.5 1.9 | **6** TH | 0518 1130 1745 | 1.9 4.4 2.1 | **21** F | 0008 0634 1250 | 4.7 1.8 4.6 | **6** SA | 0537 1145 1806 | 1.8 4.5 2.0 | **21** SU |

**2.** Tide tables showing the times and heights of high and low water at various ports around the coast can be found in both *Macmillan's* and *Reed's* nautical almanacs.

## TIMES

| TIME ZONE −0100 | FRANCE, WEST COAST - BREST | | | | |
| (French Standard Time) | | | | | |
| Subtract 1 hour for GMT | LAT 48°23'N        LONG 4°29'W | | | | |
| For French Summer Time add | TIMES AND HEIGHTS OF HIGH AND LOW WATERS | | | | |
| ONE hour in non-shaded areas | | | | | |
| MAY | | JUNE | | JULY | |
| TIME    m | TIME    m | TIME    m | TIME    m | TIME    m | TIME    m |

By far the most common cause of error in anyone's tidal calculations is a little snag arising out of the way we measure time.

In all our examples, we've referred to **GMT** – Greenwich Mean Time.

But other countries use other times, and even in Britain, we put our clocks forward in the spring so that for most of the boating season, our clock time is not GMT, but **BST** (British Summer Time). So unless we're prepared to keep a clock set to GMT, we have to add an hour to the times given by the tables: High Water Plymouth at 1933 GMT, corresponds to 2033 BST.

The time to which the tables refer is always indicated somewhere on the page of predictions, and is usually the standard time of the country concerned. French standard time, for example is shown as −0100. The minus sign indicates that you have to subtract one hour from the times shown if you want to convert back into GMT.

So if HW Brest is at 0706 (−0100) it's at 0606 GMT, or 0706 BST.

In real life, it's most convenient to keep your own watch set to the time the locals are using, so if France is using French Summer Time you can forget GMT and BST, and just add an hour to convert the tables to local clock time.

Much the same thing applies in the USA, except that time zones are often quoted as 'time meridians'. The tide tables for Boston, for example specify that the time meridian used is 75°W. In this context, every 15° is one hour, so 75°W means that Boston's Eastern Standard Time (EST) is five hours behind GMT. But all you really need to remember is to add an hour to convert the tide table time into clock time whenever daylight saving time is in operation.

---

the tide tables show that the water is now 5.4 metres above chart datum.

So in the buoyed channel, the depth is now

5.4 + 2.1 = 7.5 metres.

And the rocks, 2.7 metres above chart datum, are covered by

5.4 − 2.7 = 2.7 metres of water.

So the passage isn't really 100 yards wide as it appears on the chart – it's grown to over half a mile.

Look at almost any river estuary, and you'll find vast areas of water available to anyone who knows how to work the tide. The tide tables open up little-known creeks

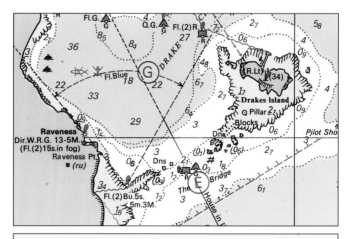

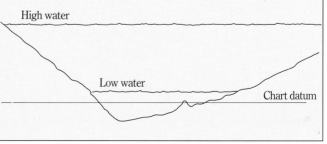

---

**3.** The passage between Drakes Island and the shore appears to be only 100 yards across on the chart, but at high water it could be half a mile wide.

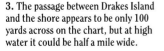

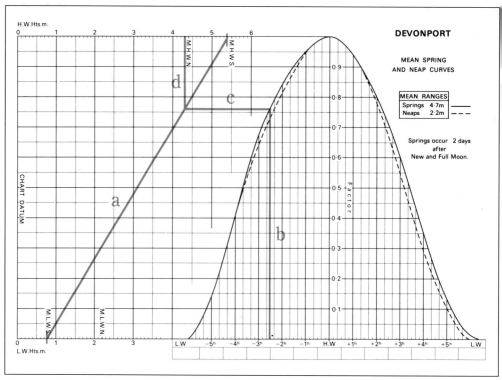

**4.** Using tidal curves to predict the height of water at a particular time (see instructions in text).

(most of which seem to have pubs at the end), give access to some of the most sheltered harbours, and take the worry out of some pretty dodgy-looking short cuts.

## INTERMEDIATE TIMES

Tide tables are quite thick enough as it is. If they were to show the height of tide for every minute of every day they'd be completely unmanageable. So they don't. They concentrate instead on the times and heights of high and low waters.

Between high and low water, you have to turn to a graph, usually on the page just before the predictions (Fig 4). It's a fairly straightforward representation of the way the water level changes as time goes by, rising from low water,

on the left hand side of the bell-shape, to high water at the centre, and back down to low water on the right.

Neap tides and spring tides don't behave in exactly the same way, so it's really two graphs in one, with a typical neap tide being shown as a dotted line.

The really clever bit is the space just to the left of the graph, which serves as a ready reckoner so that these two standard curves can cope with any tide in that particular port.

Like most clever ideas, it's very simple to use.

Suppose we want the height of tide at 1700 GMT on 16 May at Plymouth (Devonport).
1. Start by marking the height of low water (0.8m) on the scale in the bottom left-hand corner, and the height of high

water (5.4m) on the corresponding scale across the top.
2. Join the two marks with a straight line (Fig 4a).
3. Decide whether this is a spring or a neap tide. In this case, the range is 4.6m, and as the graph shows that a typical spring is 4.7m, we'll be using the spring curve.
4. Find the 'required time' under the graph. In this case, the required time is 1700 GMT, and high water is at 1933 GMT, so we are interested in 2½ hours before HW.
5. Move straight upwards from the required time, to meet the relevant (in this case spring) curve (Fig 4b).
6. Move horizontally left, to meet the pencilled line (Fig 4c).
7. Move straight upwards, to

the scale across the top of the page.

8. Read off the height of tide from the scale – in this case 4.3m (Fig 4d).

### INTERMEDIATE HEIGHTS

It may be interesting to know how much water you've got, but it's often more important to predict the time at which the water will reach a certain level.

Suppose, having got into Plymouth, we want to take the dinghy to a pub at the top of a creek. The chart shows that the creek dries 4.2 metres (Fig 5a) so if the dinghy needs 0.5m of water, we can only do it when the height of tide is greater than 4.7m (Fig 5b).

It's rather like doing the last problem in reverse, but it starts off in just the same way:

1. Start by marking the height of high and low water on the appropriate scale on the left hand side of the page.

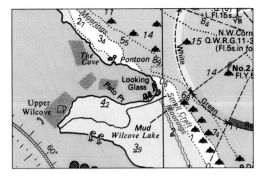

**5.** The creek at Upper Wilcove dries 4.2m, so to take a dinghy to the pub we need to calculate when the height of tide is 4.7m.

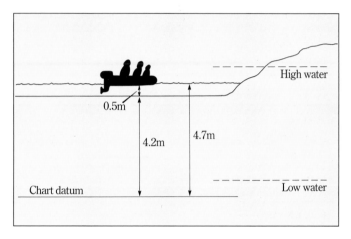

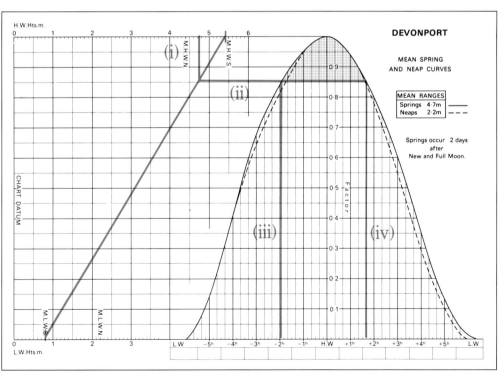

**6.** Salcombe Harbour is picturesque and very sheltered – but it doesn't warrant a full set of tide tables.

2. Join the two marks with a straight line.

3. Decide whether this is a spring or a neap tide.

Here's where it changes.

4. We know we require a height of 4.7m, so start at 4.7m on the left hand side of the page, and move down to meet the pencil line (Fig 5c-i).

5. Move across the page to meet the curve (Fig 5c-ii).

6. Move down the page to read off the time from the bottom of the page. In this case we can see that the tide will be high enough to get to and from the pub at any time from 1 hour 55 min before High water to 1 hour 40 min after (Fig 5c-iii and iv).

7. We know, from the tables, that High Water is at 1933 GMT, so we can get there at 1738 GMT, and must get away again before 2113 GMT.

### OTHER PORTS

The graph saves a lot of space, but it would still be impractical to carry tide tables for every single port. The obvious solution is to concentrate on major ports like Plymouth (Devonport).

Salcombe, twenty miles to the east, is a different sort of place altogether. It has no facilities for ships, so it doesn't warrant a full set of tidal predictions of its own. But it's a perfectly sheltered and very picturesque natural harbour, with hundreds of moorings. The only snag is that its entrance is guarded by a shallow sand bar (Fig 6).

The bar makes tidal information particularly important – and the tide tables provide it, in the form of **tidal differences** (Fig 7).

It pays to think of the differences as two separate tables, each divided into four columns, whose job is to tell us the difference between Salcombe's tides and those of Devonport.

The first two columns relate to high water, and tell us that if HW Devonport is at 0100 GMT or 1300 GMT, there

---

**SALCOMBE**   10-1-19
Devon

**CHARTS**
Admiralty 28, 1634, 1613; Stanford 13; Imray C6, Y48; OS 202

**TIDES**
−0535 Dover; ML 3.1; Duration 0615; Zone 0 (GMT).

**Standard Port DEVONPORT (←)**

| Times | | | | Height (metres) | | | |
|-------|------|------|------|------|------|------|------|
| HW | | LW | | MHWS | MHWN | MLWN | MLWS |
| 0100 | 0600 | 0100 | 0600 | 5.5 | 4.4 | 2.2 | 0.8 |
| 1300 | 1800 | 1300 | 1800 | | | | |

**Differences SALCOMBE**

| | | | | | | | |
|------|--------|--------|--------|------|------|------|------|
| 0000 | +0010 | +0005 | −0005 | −0.2 | −0.3 | −0.1 | −0.1 |

**START POINT**

| | | | | | | | |
|-------|--------|--------|--------|------|------|------|------|
| +0005 | +0030 | −0005 | +0005 | −0.2 | −0.4 | −0.1 | −0.1 |

**SHELTER**
Perfectly protected harbour but entrance is affected by S winds. The estuary is 4 M long and has 8 creeks off it, called lakes, which dry. Limited anchorage between ferry and prohibited area. Plenty of visitors deep water moorings. (Hr Mr's launch will contact − on duty 0700-2000 (LT) in season (0600-2200 (LT) in peak season) all have VHF Ch 14). There can be an uncomfortable swell with S winds in the anchorage off the town. Visitors' pontoon and moorings in the Bag are sheltered. New visitors pontoon for short stay by Hr Mr office, Whitestrand.

**7.** Tidal difference tables can be used to calculate the height of tide and the times of high and low waters in secondary ports such as Salcombe Harbour.

is a time difference of 0000. So HW Salcombe is at the same time as HW Devonport. But if HW Devonport is at 0600 GMT or 1800 GMT, HW Salcombe is ten minutes later (+0010).

On 18 May, for example, the tables for Devonport show that high water is at 0845. This is roughly mid-way between 0600 and 1300, so it would be reasonable to assume that the difference will be roughly midway between the differences given for 0600 and 1300, or +0005.

So HW Salcombe is at 0845 + 0005 = 0850 GMT.

We could be even more precise about it, and say that as 0845 is 11/28 of the way from 0600 to 1300, the difference must be 17/28 of 10 minutes, or 6 minutes – but that's crediting the tide tables with more accuracy than they deserve, so this kind of nit-picking interpolation is only worth bothering with if the figures in the difference column amount to more than an hour.

The next two difference columns relate to the time of Low water, and work in exactly the same way. LW Devonport, according to the tables, is at 1446 GMT.

If it had been at midnight or midday, the difference column tells us that LW Salcombe would be 5 minutes later, and if it had been at 0600 or 1800, 5 minutes earlier.

As 1446 is roughly half-way between 1200 and 1800, we'll take the half-way difference, or 0000.

The other half of the difference table is similar, except that it relates to heights, telling us that if HW Devonport were 5.5m, HW Salcombe would be 0.2m lower. If HW Devonport were only 4.4m, the difference would be 0.3m. The tables tell us that HW Devonport is 5.0m,

so it would seem sensible to use a difference of −0.25m, to give a height of 5.0 − 0.25 = 4.75.

Low Water, in this case, is even easier, because the difference is −0.1m regardless of the height of tide at Devonport. LW Salcombe must be 1.2 − 0.1 = 1.1m.

So out of Devonport tide tables and the Salcombe differences we've produced
0850  4.7
1446  1.1
. . . the vital data for Salcombe!

Of course, we don't have a graph, but the one for the standard port (Devonport) will serve.

## A WORD TO THE WISE

It's probably fair to say that in navigation you should work as accurately as possible, and then allow a margin for error. This is particularly true of tide tables, whose authoritative-looking rows of apparently precise data make it easy to forget that they are only predictions.

Atmospheric pressure can make a difference. High barometric pressures, which give us warm windless days in summer, press down on the sea's surface, giving tides which may be a foot or so (0.3m) lower than predicted.

The depressions that cause wind and rain tend to be shorter-lived, but they still reduce the pressure enough to allow the sea to rise. This can be exaggerated by the effect of the wind: a strong onshore wind will tend to raise the height of high water, and make it stay high for longer than the curve suggests. But if the wind is offshore, it will have the opposite effect, blowing the water away from the coast to lower the height of tide. Although tidal predictions are usually surprisingly accurate, it's wise to allow a margin for error, and in exposed waters allow an extra margin to allow for the effect of waves.

## TIDAL ANOMALIES

It's worth keeping an eye open, too, for areas with **tidal anomalies** – of which one of the best known is certainly the Solent. The Isle of Wight distorts the flow of water up and down the English Channel to such an extent that Southampton is often described as having 'Double HIgh Waters', while at Poole, High Water is a drawn-out affair lasting up to four hours, and so ill-defined that the tide tables can't quote a time of High Water at all! In practice this doesn't really pose a

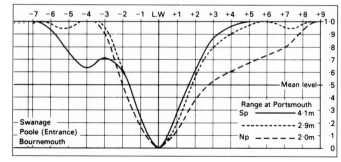

8. Tidal anomalies in the Solent produce an extended high water at Poole, so almanac publishers base their tidal curves around the time of low water.

| TIDAL PREDICTION FORM | | | | |
|---|---|---|---|---|
| STANDARD PORT **DEVONPORT** | | | SECONDARY PORT **SALCOMBE** | |
| | HIGH WATER | | LOW WATER | |
| | TIME | HEIGHT | TIME | HEIGHT |
| STANDARD PORT | 0845 | 5·0 | 1446 | 1·2 |
| DIFFERENCES | +0005 | -0·3 | 0000 | -0·1 |
| SECONDARY PORT | 0850 | 4·7 | 1446 | 1·1 |
| Correction for time zone | 0100 | | 0100 | |
| | 0950 | 4·7 | 1546 | 1·1 |

**9.** It's useful to make up a blank tidal prediction form to save time and remind you of the steps involved.

problem, because the publishers of tidal predictions have found a variety of ways of dealing with unusual situations, and invariably take great care to explain the methods they've chosen (Fig 8).

## THE CAUSES OF TIDE

Between the earth and moon there's a gravitational attraction, just strong enough to stop the moon flying off into space without being quite strong enough to pull it down into a collision with the earth. At the same time, the moon is also exerting its own attraction on the earth.

But the water nearest the moon is attracted towards the moon by a slightly stronger force, so it is pulled towards the moon slightly faster than the earth itself.

At the same time, the water further from the moon is affected by a rather weaker force, so it gets left behind.

The end result is a pair of bulges – literally 'tidal waves' – which travel round the world in step with the moon (Fig 10).

The sun is so far away that it's effect is rather less, but when it joins forces with the

moon (at full and new moon), it's enough to increase the size of the tidal waves, to create spring tides. And when it's at right angles to the earth, relative to the moon, it tends to oppose the effect of the moon, producing neap tides.

On their own, these astronomical **tide raising forces** are not enough to create big tides – in mid ocean the tidal waves probably don't amount to more than about ½ metre. But if you think of water sloshing around in a basin, you'll see that a small but rhythmic force is all that's required to produce quite substantial changes of level around the edges.

### A RULE OF THUMB

With a little practice, it's not too difficult or time-consuming to work out tidal heights properly. But there's a handy little rule that will give a reasonable approximation for most ports – but not the odd-balls such as the Solent.

Called the **Rule of Twelfths,** it says that: in the first hour after LW, the tide rises one twelfth of its range;
in the 2nd, 2/12;
in the 3rd, 3/12;
in the 4th, 3/12;
in the 5th, 2/12; and
in the 6th, 1/12.

So two hours after Low water, for example, the tide will have risen 1/12 + 2/12 = ¼ of its total range.

If Low Water was 0.8m at 1316, and the range is 4.6m, then by 1516 the height of tide should be:
0.8m (height of low water) + 1.15m (¼ of the range) = 1.95m

That's exactly what happens to the tides as they slosh around in the giant basins of the Atlantic, Pacific, and Indian oceans, although the picture is confused by the

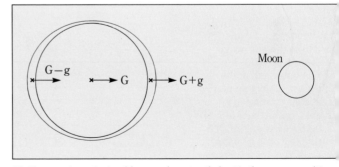

**10.** The moon's gravitational force produces two 'bulges' in the oceans, resulting in the regular rise and fall of water which we see as tides.

fact that the basins are all of different sizes, and have irregularly-shaped edges. This can produce exceptionally big tides where the tidal waves are funnelled into relatively shallow waters such as the English Channel, or distort the rhythm to produce daily (instead of half-daily) tides in the Gulf of Mexico.

## QUESTION

On 2 May, you're in Salcombe Harbour, in a boat which requires 0.9 metres of water to float. You're thinking of going for an evening drink at a pub at the head of a creek, where the chart shows a drying height of 2.4 metres.

Using the information given in Figs 2, 4, and 7, what is the earliest you can expect to get there, with a safety margin of 0.7m?

## ANSWER

Required depth
0.7m + 0.9m = 1.6m
Required height
1.6m + 2.4m = 4.0m
LW Devonport is
1338 GMT 1.4m
HW Devonport is
1939 GMT 5.1m
Differences – Salcombe
LW +0003min –0.1m
HW +0008min – 0.2m
LW Salcombe
1341 GMT = 1441 BST 1.3m
HW Salcombe
1947 GMT = 2047 BST 4.9m
From curves, height < 4.0m
from HW – 2h 30m
i.e. 1817 BST

## TIDE TABLES

THE tide tables show the height of the tide above or below chart datum (Fig 1).

Leaving Boston at 0629 EST on 16 May, for instance, a glance at the tide tables would be enough to show us that – give or take a bit to allow for weather conditions – the water should be 1.6 feet below chart datum. (The minus sign shows that we are looking at a level below chart datum).

So if we were thinking of passing over a shoal that was shown on the chart as being 6 feet deep, we could expect to find

6 – 1.6 = 4.4 feet of water.

Try the same thing a few hours later, at 1244 EST, when the tide tables show that the water will be 10.3 feet above chart datum, and over that same 6-foot shoal there should be    6 + 10.3 = 16.3 feet.

# 5

# THE AMERICAN WAY

Look at almost any river estuary, and you'll find vast areas of water available to anyone who knows how to work the tide. The tide tables open up little-known creeks, give access to some of the most sheltered anchorages, and take the worry out of some pretty dodgy-looking short cuts.

## INTERMEDIATE TIMES

Tide tables are quite thick enough as it is. If they were to show the height of tide for every minute of every day they'd be completely unmanageable. So they don't. They concentrate instead on the times and heights of high and low waters.

Between high and low water, you either have to use the Rule of Twelfths (Chapter 4), or turn to a **Rise and Fall of Tide table,** usually printed just before the main tide tables (Fig 2). Both methods are based on the assumption that the tide takes exactly six hours to rise and fall, and that it does so with perfect, mathematical precision. Neither of these is true, but for most purposes either method is close enough, especially as a prudent navigator will allow a generous safety margin.

Suppose we want to know the height of tide at Boston at 1000 EST on 16 May.
1. Start by working out the range of tide. That's the difference between high and low water: 11.9 feet.
2. Look for the most appropriate vertical column – in this case it's the one headed 12 feet.

## BOSTON, MASS.

### TIME MERIDIAN 75°W
### ADD 1 HOUR FOR DAYLIGHT SAVING TIME                    HIGH

| | MAY | | | | JUNE | | | | JULY | | |
|---|---|---|---|---|---|---|---|---|---|---|---|
| | Time h.min. | Ht. ft. | Time h.min. | Ht. ft. | Time h.min. | Ht. ft. | Time h.min. | Ht. ft. | Time h.min. | Ht. ft. | Time h.min. | Ht. ft. |
| **1** 0016 10.5 | | **16** 0000 12.0 | | **1** 0114 10.0 | | **16** 0135 11.7 | | **1** 0130 10.0 | | **16** 0212 11.1 | |
| 0640 −0.1 | | 0629 −1.6 | | 0738 0.5 | | 0759 −1.3 | | 0749 0.4 | | 0827 −0.8 | |
| W 1253 9.2 | | Th 1244 10.3 | | Sa 1354 8.8 | | Su 1418 10.4 | | M 1404 9.2 | | Tu 1447 10.7 | |
| 1846 1.1 | | 1841 −0.1 | | 1946 1.6 | | 2017 0.0 | | 2003 1.3 | | 2054 −0.1 | |
| **2** 0056 10.3 | | **17** 0053 11.9 | | **2** 0157 9.8 | | **17** 0232 11.2 | | **2** 0212 9.8 | | **17** 0308 10.4 | |
| 0719 0.2 | | 0722 −1.4 | | 0820 0.6 | | 0853 −0.9 | | 0831 0.6 | | 0918 −0.2 | |
| Th 1335 9.0 | | F 1337 10.2 | | Su 1436 8.8 | | M 1513 10.4 | | Tu 1444 9.3 | | W 1540 10.5 | |
| 1928 1.4 | | 1935 0.0 | | 2031 1.7 | | 2116 0.2 | | 2048 1.3 | | 2150 0.3 | |
| **3** 0138 10.0 | | **18** 0149 11.6 | | **3** 0242 9.6 | | **18** 0331 10.6 | | **3** 0255 9.5 | | **18** 0403 9.7 | |
| 0804 0.5 | | 0817 −1.1 | | 0903 0.8 | | 0947 −0.3 | | 0911 0.6 | | 1011 0.5 | |
| F 1418 8.7 | | Sa 1434 10.0 | | M 1519 8.8 | | Tu 1610 10.3 | | W 1526 9.4 | | Th 1633 10.2 | |
| 2012 1.6 | | 2032 0.3 | | 2119 1.8 | | 2217 0.5 | | 2134 1.2 | | 2249 0.7 | |
| **4** 0223 9.7 | | **19** 0246 11.1 | | **4** 0327 9.4 | | **19** 0432 10.0 | | **4** 0341 9.3 | | **19** 0503 9.1 | |
| 0847 0.8 | | 0913 −0.7 | | 0948 1.0 | | 1042 0.2 | | 0957 0.8 | | 1103 1.0 | |
| Sa 1503 8.5 | | Su 1534 9.9 | | Tu 1604 8.9 | | W 1707 10.2 | | Th 1611 9.6 | | F 1728 9.9 | |
| 2059 1.9 | | 2132 0.6 | | 2209 1.8 | | 2318 0.7 | | 2227 1.1 | | 2349 0.9 | |
| **5** 0311 9.4 | | **20** 0348 10.6 | | **5** 0417 9.1 | | **20** 0533 9.4 | | **5** 0433 9.1 | | **20** 0603 8.6 | |
| 0936 1.1 | | 1011 −0.3 | | 1034 1.1 | | 1138 0.7 | | 1044 0.9 | | 1159 1.5 | |
| Su 1553 8.4 | | M 1634 9.8 | | W 1651 9.1 | | Th 1803 10.1 | | F 1659 9.9 | | Sa 1825 9.7 | |
| 2148 2.1 | | 2235 0.8 | | 2302 1.6 | | — | | 2321 0.9 | | — | |
| **6** 0401 9.1 | | **21** 0452 10.1 | | **6** 0509 9.0 | | **21** 0022 0.8 | | **6** 0527 9.0 | | **21** 0052 1.1 | |
| 1026 1.3 | | 1110 0.2 | | 1123 1.1 | | 0635 9.0 | | 1135 1.0 | | 0704 8.3 | |

**1.** Tide tables, like these for Boston, show the times of high and low water, and their heights above or below chart datum, for every day of the year.

| h. min. | RANGE OF THE TIDE IN FEET | | | | | | | | | | | | | | |
|---|---|---|---|---|---|---|---|---|---|---|---|---|---|---|---|
| | 2 | 4 | 6 | 8 | 10 | 12 | 14 | 16 | 18 | 20 | 22 | 24 | 26 | 28 | 30 |
| 0 20 | 0.0 | 0.0 | 0.0 | 0.1 | 0.1 | 0.1 | 0.1 | 0.1 | 0.1 | 0.2 | 0.2 | 0.2 | 0.2 | 0.2 | 0.2 |
| 0 40 | 0.1 | 0.1 | 0.2 | 0.2 | 0.3 | 0.4 | 0.4 | 0.5 | 0.6 | 0.6 | 0.7 | 0.7 | 0.8 | 0.8 | 0.9 |
| 1 00 | 0.1 | 0.3 | 0.4 | 0.5 | 0.7 | 0.8 | 0.9 | 1.1 | 1.2 | 1.3 | 1.5 | 1.6 | 1.7 | 1.8 | 2.0 |
| 1 20 | 0.2 | 0.5 | 0.7 | 0.9 | 1.1 | 1.4 | 1.6 | 1.9 | 2.1 | 2.3 | 2.6 | 2.8 | 3.0 | 3.3 | 3.5 |
| 1 40 | 0.4 | 0.7 | 1.1 | 1.4 | 1.8 | 2.1 | 2.5 | 2.9 | 3.2 | 3.6 | 3.9 | 4.3 | 4.6 | 5.0 | 5.4 |
| 2 00 | 0.5 | 1.0 | 1.5 | 2.0 | 2.5 | 3.0 | 3.5 | 4.0 | 4.5 | 5.0 | 5.5 | 6.0 | 6.5 | 7.0 | 7.5 |
| 2 20 | 0.7 | 1.3 | 2.0 | 2.6 | 3.3 | 3.9 | 4.6 | 5.3 | 5.9 | 6.6 | 7.2 | 7.9 | 8.6 | 9.2 | 9.9 |
| 2 40 | 0.8 | 1.7 | 2.5 | 3.3 | 4.1 | 5.0 | 5.8 | 6.6 | 7.4 | 8.3 | 9.1 | 9.9 | 10.7 | 11.6 | 12.4 |
| 3 00 | 1.0 | 2.0 | 3.0 | 4.0 | 5.0 | 6.0 | 7.0 | 8.0 | 9.0 | 10.0 | 11.0 | 12.0 | 13.0 | 14.0 | 15.0 |
| 3 20 | 1.2 | 2.3 | 3.5 | 4.7 | 5.9 | 7.0 | 8.2 | 9.4 | 10.6 | 11.7 | 12.9 | 14.1 | 15.3 | 16.4 | 17.6 |
| 3 40 | 1.3 | 2.7 | 4.0 | 5.4 | 6.7 | 8.1 | 9.4 | 10.7 | 12.1 | 13.4 | 14.8 | 16.1 | 17.4 | 18.8 | 20.1 |
| 4 00 | 1.5 | 3.0 | 4.5 | 6.0 | 7.5 | 9.0 | 10.5 | 12.0 | 13.5 | 15.0 | 16.5 | 18.0 | 19.5 | 21.0 | 22.5 |
| 4 20 | 1.6 | 3.3 | 4.9 | 6.6 | 8.2 | 9.9 | 11.5 | 13.1 | 14.8 | 16.4 | 18.1 | 19.7 | 21.4 | 23.0 | 24.6 |
| 4 40 | 1.8 | 3.5 | 5.3 | 7.1 | 8.9 | 10.6 | 12.4 | 14.1 | 15.9 | 17.7 | 19.4 | 21.2 | 23.0 | 24.7 | 26.5 |
| 5 00 | 1.9 | 3.7 | 5.6 | 7.5 | 9.3 | 11.2 | 13.1 | 14.9 | 16.8 | 18.7 | 20.5 | 22.4 | 24.3 | 26.1 | 28.0 |
| 5 20 | 1.9 | 3.9 | 5.8 | 7.8 | 9.7 | 11.6 | 13.6 | 15.5 | 17.5 | 19.4 | 21.3 | 23.3 | 25.2 | 27.2 | 29.1 |
| 5 40 | 2.0 | 4.0 | 6.0 | 7.9 | 9.9 | 11.9 | 13.9 | 15.9 | 17.9 | 19.8 | 21.8 | 23.8 | 25.8 | 27.8 | 29.8 |
| 6 00 | 2.0 | 4.0 | 6.0 | 8.0 | 10.0 | 12.0 | 14.0 | 16.0 | 18.0 | 20.0 | 22.0 | 24.0 | 26.0 | 28.0 | 30.0 |

**2.** Rise and Fall of Tide tables can be used to calculate the height of tide at times between high and low water.

3. Work out how long the tide has been rising. In this case, low water was at 0629 EST and we are interested in 1000 EST, so it has been rising for 3 hours 31 minutes.

4. Find the nearest time in the left hand column, and run across the table to read off the answer where the time row crosses the range column. Here, we have a choice of two

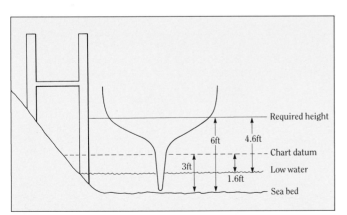

**3.** The chart shows only 3 feet of water alongside the dock, but we need 6 feet to float. That's 3 feet over chart datum. Low water today is 1.6 feet below chart datum, so we need 4.6 feet over low water. Drawing a sketch like this will often clarify the problem.

possible time rows: 3 hours 20 minutes or 3 hours 40 minutes. It makes sense to choose the most pessimistic (3 hours 20 minutes), giving an answer of 7.0 feet.
5. That is the height of tide above low water, but low water is 1.6 feet below chart datum, so at 1000 EST the water will be $7.0 - 1.6 = 5.4$ feet above chart datum.

## INTERMEDIATE HEIGHTS

It may be interesting to know how much water you've got, but it's often more important to predict the time at which the water will reach a certain level.

Suppose we want to call at a dock where the chart shows only 3 feet of water at chart datum, but that our boat draws 6 feet. So we can only get there when the height of tide is more than 3 feet (Fig 3).

It's rather like doing the last problem in reverse, but it starts off in just the same way:
1. Start by working out the range of tide: 11.9 feet.
2. Look for the most appropriate vertical column: the one headed 12 feet.

Here's where it changes.
3. We know we require a height of 3 feet above chart datum, but the rise and fall table refers to heights above low water. Low water, in this case, is 1.6 feet below chart datum, so 3 feet above chart datum is 4.6 feet above low water.
4. Move down the 12 feet column to find a height of more than 4.6 feet.
5. Move across that row, and read off the corresponding time in the left hand column. In this case, the tide will reach 5.0 feet, 2 hours 40 minutes after low water.
6. We know, from the tables, that low water is at 0629 EST, so we can get to the dock at 0909 EST.

| 10:44 | TIDAL DIFFERENCES on BOSTON, MASS | | | | | |
|---|---|---|---|---|---|---|
| | POSITION | | DIFFERENCES | | | |
| | | | Time | | Height | |
| PLACE | Lat. | Long. | High water | Low water | High water | Low water |
| | ° ′ N. | ° ′ W. | h. m. | h. m. | feet | feet |
| **MASSACHUSETTS, Outer Coast** Time meridian, 75°W. | | | | | | |
| **Nantucket Sound, North Side** | | | | | | |
| Stage Harbor | 41 40 | 69 58 | +0 57 | +0 48 | *0.41 | *0.41 |
| Wychmere Harbor | 41 40 | 70 04 | +0 52 | +0 25 | *0.39 | *0.39 |
| Dennis Port | 41 39 | 70 07 | +1 03 | +0 38 | *0.36 | *0.36 |
| South Yarmouth, Bass River | 41 40 | 70 11 | +1 48 | +1 46 | *0.29 | *0.29 |
| Hyannis Port | 41 38 | 70 18 | +1 03 | +0 31 | *0.32 | *0.32 |
| Cotuit Highlands | 41 36 | 70 26 | +1 17 | +0 47 | *0.26 | *0.26 |
| Poponesset Island, Poponesset Bay | 41 35 | 70 28 | +2 03 | +1 52 | *0.24 | *0.24 |
| Succonnesset Point | 41 33 | 70 29 | +0 54 | +0 39 | *0.20 | *0.20 |

**4.** Tidal difference tables are used to work out the heights and times of high and low water at smaller harbours by referring to the predictions for a nearby standard port.

## OTHER PORTS

It is still impractical to carry tide tables for every single port. The obvious solution is to concentrate on major ports like Boston, and to use **tidal differences** (Fig 4) to fill in the details of places such as Stage Harbor.

The difference tables are divided into six separate columns – of which the first two give the latitude and longitude of the place in question.

The next two tell us the time difference between Stage Harbor's tides and those of Boston: high water at Stage Harbor is +57 and low water is +48. Applying these to the times of high and low water at Boston gives:

HW 1244 + 57 = 1341
LW 0629 + 48 = 0717

In this case, high water at Stage Harbor is later than at Boston, the plus sign showing that the difference has to be added. If local high water occurs before high water at Boston, a minus sign would be used to show that the difference should be subtracted.

The next two columns refer to heights, but although they look similar, they work in a different way. At Stage

Harbor the differences for high and low water are both given as *0.41. The * signifies that this is a ratio: in other words, high water at Stage Harbor is 0.41 as high as high water at Boston:

10.3 × 0.41 = 4.2
and −1.6 × 0.41 = −0.6

So out of the Boston tide tables and the Stage Harbor differences we've produced

0717   −0.6
1341    4.2

. . . the vital data for Stage Harbor.

Intermediate times and heights can be calculated from this, using the rule of twelfths

or rise and fall of tide tables – exactly as they were for Boston itself.

## TIDAL CURRENTS

The way **tidal currents** (called tidal streams in the UK) are shown in US publications is also slightly different to their counterparts in the UK.

In many areas, the tide flows first in one direction, then in another. As only two directions are involved, the necessary information can be presented in tables (Fig 5).

These **current tables** look very much like the tide tables, except that they have three columns of entries for each day of the year.

The first column shows the times of slack water – when the tidal current is just about to change direction.

The next column shows the times when the tidal currents will be at their greatest, with the third column showing what that rate will be – letters E (for ebb) and F (for flood) showing whether it's an inward or outward flowing current. A note at the top of the page shows the direction of the flood and ebb currents.

| 10:84 | **CURRENT TABLES** | | | | | | | | | | |
|---|---|---|---|---|---|---|---|---|---|---|---|

**THE RACE — LONG ISLAND SOUND**
F–FLOOD, DIR. 295° TRUE          E–EBB, DIR. 100° TRUE

| | | MAY | | | | | | JUNE | | |
|---|---|---|---|---|---|---|---|---|---|---|
| | Slack Water h.min. | Maximum Current h.min. knots | | | Slack Water h.min. | Maximum Current h.min. knots | | | Slack Water h.min. | Maximum Current h.min. knots | |
| **1** W | 0031 0724 1306 1926 | 0404 1000 1624 2207 | 3.4E 2.6F 2.7E 2.5F | **16** Th | 0023 0708 1301 1918 | 0350 0953 1618 2213 | 4.5E 3.7F 3.8E 3.7F | **1** Sa | 0123 0817 1403 2026 | 0458 1055 1724 2308 | 3.0E 2.4F 2.4E 2.2F |
| **2** Th | 0110 0805 1347 2008 | 0445 1041 1707 2250 | 3.2E 2.4F 2.5E 2.3F | **17** F | 0117 0802 1357 2018 | 0446 1049 1714 2308 | 4.4E 3.6F 3.7E 3.5F | **2** Su | 0205 0856 1446 2113 | 0541 1138 1809 2353 | 2.8E 2.3F 2.4E 2.1F |
| **3** F | 0151 0848 1431 2055 | 0528 1123 1756 2337 | 2.9E 2.2F 2.3E 2.1F | **18** Sa | 0214 0900 1455 2123 | 0543 1146 1815 — | 4.2E 3.5F 3.6E — | **3** M | 0250 0938 1531 2205 | 0622 1225 1858 — | 2.6E 2.3F 2.4E — |
| **4** | 0236 0934 | 0616 1209 | 2.7E 2.1E | **19** | — 0315 | 0009 0644 | 3.3F 3.9E | **4** | 0340 0714 | 0045 0714 | 2.0F 2.5E |

**5.** Tidal current tables predict the times of slack water and maximum flow, along with the maximum rate of the current.

So the tables in Fig 5 are telling us that on 16 May at The Race in Long Island Sound there will be
slack water at 0023 EST
an ebb current of 4.5 knots at 0350 EST,
slack water at 0708 EST
a flood current of 3.7 knots at 0953 EST
slack water at 1301 EST – and so on.

There is so much information here that it's very easy to make a quick estimate of the tidal current at any moment in time. At 0830 EST, for instance, the current will be flooding, and starting to build up towards its maximum of 3.7 knots – so we could guess that it might be about 1.8 knots.

If you want to be more accurate than this, you can do it with the **Rule of thirds.**

This says that: one hour before or after slack water, the tidal current is one third of its maximum rate, 2 hours before or after it's ⅔, and 3 hours before or after it's ¾.

## CURRENT DIFFERENCES

It's not much good knowing all about the tidal currents in The Race if you happen to be somewhere else! And unfortunately you only need to move a few hundred yards away to find a completely different tidal current. To get round this problem, the tidal current tables include pages of **current differences,** very much like those used for working out tidal heights.

Those in commercially-produced almanacs (Fig 6) may only show the time difference of slack water, maximum flood, and maximum ebb; but regular NOAA tables include ratios – showing how much stronger or weaker you can expect the maximum current to be.

Finding the necessary

| | | | | | | | | 10:51 |
|---|---|---|---|---|---|---|---|---|
| **CURRENT DIFFERENCES on BOSTON HARBOR, MASS.** | | | | | | | | |
| | | | POSITION | | TIME DIFFERENCES | | | |
| PLACE | | | Lat. | Long | Min. before Flood | Flood | Min. before Ebb | Ebb |
| **MASSACHUSETTS COAST** Time Meridian 75°W. | | | ° ′ N. | ° ′ W. | h. m. | h. m. | h. m. | h. m. |
| Merrimack River entrance | | | 42 49 | 70 48 | + 1 04 | + 1 15 | + 1.13 | − 0.34 |
| Newburyport, Merrimack River | | | 42 48 | 70 52 | + 1 28 | + 1 48 | + 1.47 | + 0.35 |
| Plum Island Sound entrance | | | 42 42 | 70 47 | + 0 36 | + 0 50 | + 0.48 | − 0.07 |
| Annisquam Harbor Lt. | | | 42 40 | 70 41 | + 0 42 | + 0 49 | + 0.58 | + 0.03 |
| Gloucester Harbor entrance | | | 42 34 | 70 40 | − 0 28 | + 0 01 | − 0.29 | − 0.36 |
| Blyman Canal ent., Gloucester Harbor | | | 42 36 | 70 40 | − 0 06 | + 0 05 | − 0.15 | − 0.39 |
| Marblehead Channel | | | 42 30 | 70 49 | + 1 09 | + 1 09 | + 1.09 | + 1.09 |
| Nahant, 0.4 n.mi. E of East Point | | | 42 25 | 70 53 | + 0 04 | − 0 41 | + 0.15 | + 0.22 |
| Pea Island, 0.4 n.mi. SE of | | | 42 24 | 70 54 | + 0 53 | + 0 55 | + 0.42 | − 0.01 |
| Bass Point, 1.2 n.mi. SE of | | | 42 24 | 70 55 | − 0 22 | + 1 20 | + 0.58 | − 0.14 |

**6.** Current difference tables – these are from *Reed's Nautical Almanac and Coast Pilot* – are used rather like the tidal difference tables to predict the times of slack water and maximum flow.

information and working it all out can be very tedious and time consuming – especially as the positions shown in the current tables are not identified on charts.

Fortunately, there is an easier way – **tidal current charts** – very much like British tidal stream atlases we mentioned in Chapter 2!

## TIDAL CURRENT CHARTS

Like their British counterparts, American tidal current charts (Fig 7) show the tidal currents pictorially, with a separate chart for each hour

of the tidal cycle.

The big difference is that they show only the rate of current at spring tides – not at neaps. You can easily estimate the rates on smaller tides by looking back to the current tables. If the current tables show a maximum rate during spring tides of, say, 4.8 knots, but on the day you're interested the rate in the tables is 3.6 knots, then today's currents are only 75% of the maximum. So you should multiply the rates given in the tidal current chart by 75% to find what the currents are up to today.

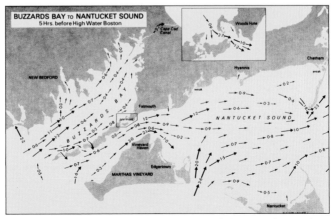

**7.** Tidal current charts like these from *Reed's Nautical Almanac and Coast Pilot* show the tidal currents pictorially for each hour of the tidal cycle.

NAVIGATION isn't solely concerned with finding out where you are and knowing where you're going. It's also about not bumping into things along the way.

These two aspects of the job acquire different priorities in different places: offshore, where there's deep water all around, the first is of over-riding importance. Close inshore, especially in or near a harbour, knowing where you're going is less of a problem: navigation then becomes much more concerned with avoiding the rocks and shoals that line your route.

At the same time, of course,

# 6
# PILOTAGE ON THE PLANE

## BUOYAGE

The most obvious aids to pilotage are the **buoys** and **beacons** that mark channels and hazards (Fig 1).

Their shapes, colours, and topmarks combine to form an elaborate code (see page 50), giving vital information at a glance to anyone who has taken the trouble to learn what they mean.

Even so, they have their shortcomings: in particular, they can't tell you anything about the actual depth of water. Many channels are marked even though they dry out at low tide, so you certainly can't assume that

**1.** Minor channels are often marked by posts called beacons.

you'll be concerned with avoiding other traffic, getting ready to go alongside or pick up a mooring, and quite possibly wanting to look around at the passing scenery as well.

This calls for a different set of navigation techniques, together known as **pilotage.**

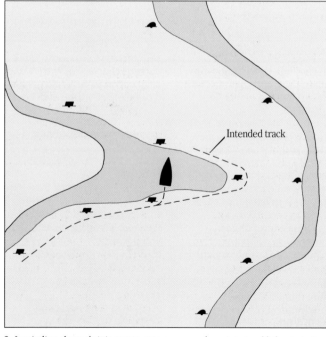

Intended track

**2.** In winding channels it is easy to cut a corner and run into trouble by aiming for the next-but-one buoy instead of the next one. (The buoyage system shown is European.)

following a buoyed channel is enough to stop you going aground. You still need to look at the chart and work out the height of tide!

Conversely, in major harbours, buoys are often laid for the benefit of ships which need ten metres of water or more just to stay afloat. There may well be plenty of water for small craft outside the marked channel, in which case it's better to avoid mixing it with the big boys.

But you can only tell by looking at the chart.

Such things aside, navigating in a well-marked channel is usually pretty straightforward – it's just a question of leaving each mark in turn on the correct side.

There are just two problems to watch out for, of which by far the most common is the straightforward risk of making a mistake. In an intricate, winding channel it's very easy to get mixed up, and cut a critical corner by aiming for the next-but-one buoy instead of the next one (Fig 2).

The cure is simple: make sure to plan your pilotage carefully in advance, noting down the bearing and distance of each mark from the one before.

That way, as soon as you reach a buoy, you know immediately where to look for the next. The distance is useful, because it helps to know whether you should be looking for a buoy fifty yards ahead or two miles away.

The other problem is caused by the effects of wind and tide. At typical harbour speeds of six or eight knots their effects are particularly pronounced, and a planing motor cruiser may well make more leeway than an equivalent sailing yacht. But if a sailing boat goes aground it rarely dents any more than her skipper's pride.

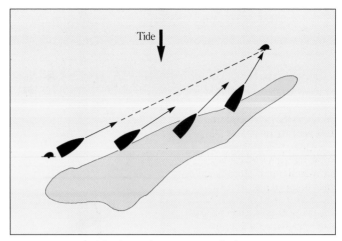

**3a.** Sometimes aiming for the next buoy is not enough: the tide sweeping across a buoyed channel could take you onto a mud bank.

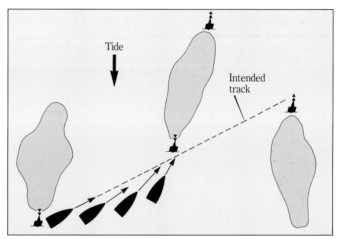

**3b.** If the tide pushes you off course you could find yourself heading for the wrong buoy.

Figures 3a and b show the problem. The solution is to look beyond the buoy you're aiming for, and pick out some convenient landmark directly beyond it. This can be anything: a house, a crane, a tree – even a parked car or sleeping cow, depending on where you happen to be. The important thing is that once any two objects appear to be in line, you've got a **transit.**

In Chapter 3 I described a transit as one of the most useful of all position lines. In this instance, however, we're not using it as part of a fix, but as a direct visual indication of the straight line that leads to the next buoy.

So if the buoy appears to slide to the left of our chosen back-marker, we need to steer left to get back on track – and vice versa (Fig 4).

## TRANSITS

The simplicity and precision of transits makes them a particularly powerful pilotage technique, especially in rocky waters, where channels are often deep but narrow, and not likely to move around from one year to the next.

A convenient transit – often called a leading line – may be formed by conspicuous buildings ashore, or by painted marks on rocks or walls, or by beacons set up for the purpose. Such transits are usually marked quite clearly on the chart (Fig 5). Unfortunately they are often much less obvious in real life, so it's worth carrying a pair of binoculars to help pick out a transit that may be formed by nothing more than a pair of painted telegraph poles or flimsy-looking lattice towers.

## CLEARING LINES

In wide channels, the precision of a transit is unnecessary. By confining all the traffic onto a

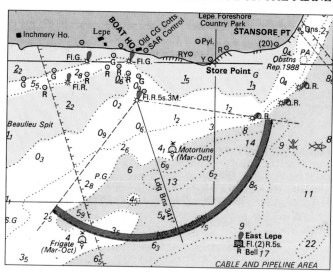

5a. The chart shows the beacons leading into Beaulieu river . . .

very narrow track, it may even be a drawback.

There may, however be several other transits available, even though they're not quite so clearly marked on the chart (Fig 5). There's one, for example, when the light beacon is in line with the pylon on Store Point.

4. Keeping the mark lined up with some fixed object ashore will ensure you follow a straight track.

But this one's different: it certainly doesn't indicate a particularly advisable route. What it does do is indicate the northern edge of the 'safe' water. As long as we can see the pylon to the right of the beacon, we know we're OK; if the two are in line we're right on the limit; while if it is to the left of the beacon we know we're uncomfortably close to the unmarked shallows of Beaulieu Spit.

A position line like this, which just clears a hazard, is called a **clearing line.** And it doesn't have to be a transit.

In this particular case, we could use a bearing. If we were right on the edge of the safe water, the bearing of the beacon would be $050°$ (M): if it increased, we'd be perilously close to the Spit.

This is a particularly useful technique when you're following any wide or funnel-shaped channel towards a single conspicuous landmark, especially as the steering compass then serves as an instant (and reasonably accurate) method of checking the bearing.

But there are plenty of

**5b.** . . . but transits are not always as obvious in real life – here the back mark is high in the trees.

deep channel, a red light if you're off to port, and a green light if you're off to starboard (Fig 6).

## PLANNING PILOTAGE

All this business of working out tidal heights, looking for suitable landmarks, and measuring bearings and distances, takes time. And if you don't have time to do all that at sea, you certainly won't be able to do it in pilotage waters, where a rock or sandbank may be just seconds away. Slowing down or stopping might give you a breathing space, but not much more: the wind and tide will still be doing their stuff. A couple of knots of tide alone could move you 60 yards in less than a minute!

So advance planning is vital.

The first part of the job is to get some kind of 'feel' for the place you're going to. Will it be a matter of driving between the pier heads, or groping your way up a winding estuary with

other possibilities. A clearing line is no more than a pre-planned position line, so you can use anything that will provide an ordinary position line. Just to recap on Chapter 3, these include:

- compass bearings
- transits
- echo sounder
- radar

and if you're really desperate:

- distance off
- electronic aids.

A variation on the theme of clearing lines is provided by **sectored lights,** though these are obviously only of any use when they are lit – at night. As the name suggests, they are arranged so that the light is only visible from certain directions – like the one indicated by an arc of red in Fig 5, which is only visible once you're in the 'safe' approach sector.

More sophisticated versions show several

different colours, usually arranged so that you see a white light if you're in the

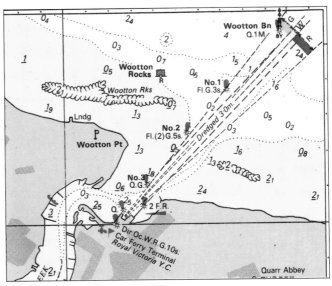

**6.** If the white light is in view, you're in the deep-water channel as you enter Wootton creek. If you see a red light, steer to starboard: if green, steer to port.

a five-knot tide sluicing through it? And is it big or small, deep or shallow, well-marked or a matter of guesswork?

The next task is to work out the height of tide at the time you expect to arrive. This is absolutely essential if there's a shallow bar across the harbour entrance that requires a minimum height of tide before you can cross it, or if there's a low bridge that you can't get under if there's too much water. Even if there are neither of these to contend with, knowing the height of tide is useful.

Even if you don't know when you expect to arrive, it's still possible to do at least part of the calculation in advance, or to work out the height of

tide for several different times an hour or two either side of your ETA.

Having assembled the most vital information you can start making a more detailed plan, by picking a suitable route and noting the necessary clearing lines, transits, buoys and beacons. For all but the most straightforward pilotage, it's a good idea to jot them down on a note pad, as well as marking them on the chart itself.

Perhaps the most tricky bit is deciding exactly where the pilotage plan should start – in other words where pilotage takes over from navigation. This sounds academic, but it can be quite important.

Coming into Portsmouth from the west, for example (Fig 7), there is a choice of

three possible routes, but the two most direct ones both involve picking up transit marks leading between the sandbanks outside the entrance.

There's no point swilling around two miles offshore looking for marks which – without local knowledge – might be difficult to identify. But it would be downright reckless to go rushing headlong towards the shallows with no more than a vague hope of recognising the transit in time.

So, despite appearances, the transits are not the start of the pilotage. What's needed is a clearing line that will allow us to go close enough to be sure of seeing the marks, while keeping far enough west to

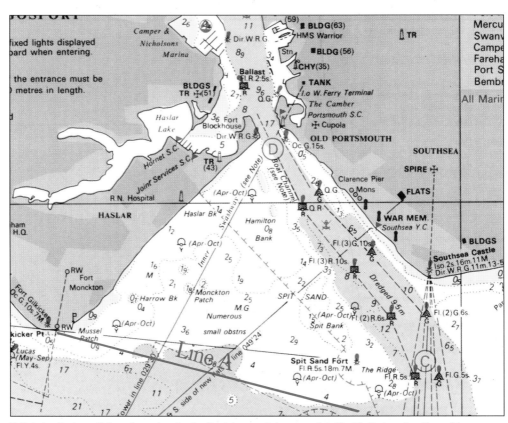

**7.** Entering Portsmouth from the west, a clearing line lets you get close enough to identify the transits with confidence.

## LOCAL KNOWLEDGE

avoid the bank. There are several possibilities.

We could, for instance, decide not to allow the bearing of Gilkicker Point to reduce to less than 290° Magnetic (line A in Fig 7).

### LOCAL KNOWLEDGE

It's quite possible to draw up a perfectly workable pilotage plan on the basis of chart and tide tables alone.

Putting such a plan into practice, however, can be a nerve-wracking experience when you wonder whether the mark you're looking at really is the one shown on the chart.

Fortunately, you can often buy a bit more 'local knowledge' in advance, in the form of the many **pilot books** (or sailing directions) published especially for yachtsmen (Fig 8). Their style and content vary enormously:

some are little more than tourist guides, others go into painstaking detail about channels that even the locals don't know about. But as far as it's possible to generalise, a good pilot book will include a description of the harbour and its approaches, a potted 'plan' of at least one route into it,

**8.** Pilots vary greatly in detail and form. Choose one that suits your requirements.

and a summary of the facilities available once you've arrived. They are usually illustrated with sketch charts and – most useful of all – with drawings or photographs of key features. The information they provide is so valuable that it's well worth making an effort to choose a pilot that suits your purposes and that you feel presents its information in the most logical and accessible way.

Perhaps the biggest drawback of any pilot – especially a good one – is that it begs to be propped up on the chart table and used as a set of instructions, rather than as a source of information.

But even the best pilot book is no substitute for a proper pilotage plan. Not for nothing do ships' log books read 'Helm and engines to Master's orders and pilot's advice'. If the captain of a ship can't hand over responsibility to a pilot standing beside him on the bridge, the skipper of a motor boat certainly can't pass the buck to the author of a book!

## BUOYS AND BEACONS: IALA A

This system of buoyage, known as IALA A, is used throughout the world, with the exception of North and South America and parts of the Far East.

It's really made up of two different, but complementary systems.

**Lateral marks** are used to mark the sides of channels.

Those on the port side of the channel when entering harbour are red, and are either can-shaped or carry a red can-shaped or cylindrical topmark. At night, some of the most important show a red flashing light (Fig 9a).

Those on the starboard side of the channel are green, and either conical or fitted with a conical topmark. At night, they show a green flashing light (Fig 9b).

Lateral marks are not always used in pairs: in fact, you'll often come across a lateral mark on its own, sometimes in a position which does not seem to relate to any clearly-defined channel. In this case it relates to the general direction of buoyage – which is clockwise around continental land-masses. This is usually pretty obvious, but if there's likely to be any doubt about it, the general direction is marked on the chart (Fig 9c).

**Cardinal marks** are used to show deep water around hazards, and are named according to the four cardinal points of the compass. So you'll find deep water by passing north of a North cardinal, east of an East cardinal, and so on.

The shape of a cardinal

**9a.** When entering harbour in Europe, leave red lateral marks to port . . .

**9b.** . . . and leave green lateral marks to starboard.

mark is irrelevant, though most are pillar buoys like those in the photographs. What's important is the shape of its topmark, and the layout of its black and yellow bands (Fig 10).

Although the permutations

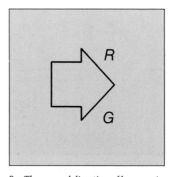

**9c.** The general direction of buoyage is sometimes shown on the chart.

of shape and colour may seem difficult, they follow a very logical pattern:
- A **North cardinal** has a topmark of two cones pointing upward – towards the top of the chart! And the cones also indicate the black bit of the buoy – at the top.
- A **South cardinal** has a topmark of two cones pointing downwards, towards the bottom of the chart, and indicating that the black band is at the bottom.
- A **West cardinal** is a little more difficult, but it might help if you remember that its cones point together, giving a 'waisted' silhouette. Again, the cones point to the black band: in the middle.
- An **East cardinal** has the only remaining option: its cones point away from each other, showing that the black parts of the buoy are at the top and bottom.

Like lateral buoys, important cardinal buoys are often fitted with lights. They're always white, and flash like the striking of a clock. So an East cardinal, at three o'clock, gives three flashes in quick succession; a South cardinal, at six o'clock gives six, and a West cardinal at nine o'clock gives nine. The North cardinal, at twelve o'clock, flashes continuously.

There's just one exception to this 'clock rule' though: because sailors aren't supposed to be able to count, they might have problems telling the difference between a South and a West, so the South is distinguished by having an extra long flash tagged onto the end of its six.

These two main types of marks are supplemented by a variety of other buoys used for special purposes.

**Isolated danger marks** are used, as the name suggests, to mark a hazard that is completely surrounded

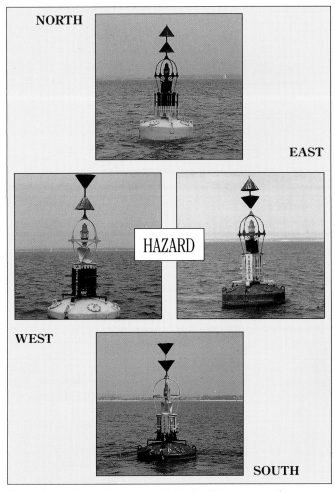

**10.** Cardinal marks (clockwise from top): North – deep water to north; East – deep water to east; South – deep water to south; West – deep water to west.

by navigable water. Even so, it doesn't pay to go too close to one without looking at the chart: the hazard might be bigger than you think!

Like a cardinal mark, its shape is irrelevant. It's the topmark of two black balls, and the pattern of black and red bands that are important. The two black balls serve as a reminder that the light – if it has one – shows groups of two white flashes (Fig 11).

**Safe water marks** are used to mark the centre line of a particularly important channel or, more often, to serve as a useful waypoint marker at the start of a buoyed channel which extends a long way offshore. They have red and white vertical stripes, and a topmark of a single red ball (Fig 12).

Finally, there is a crop of **special marks,** used to indicate things such as dumping grounds, military exercise areas, areas set aside for swimming or water skiing, or yacht racing marks.

They are invariably yellow, and may show a yellow light, but they can be any shape. If they are can or conical they are intended to be treated as though they are lateral marks of the same shape (Fig 13).

**11.** Isolated danger marks have a topmark of two black balls and a pattern of black and red bands.

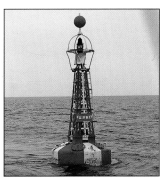

**12.** Safe water marks have a red ball topmark and red and white vertical stripes.

**13.** Special marks are always yellow but come in a variety of shapes.

## BUOYS AND BEACONS: IALA B

North and South America and parts of the Far East have adopted a similar system known as IALA B.

The cardinal marks, isolated danger marks, safe water marks, and special marks are the same in both A and B systems, although they are nowhere near as common in the USA as they are around Europe.

The really major difference is that the colours of the lateral buoys marking the sides of channels are reversed!

Those on the port side of the channel when entering harbour are green, and are either can-shaped or carry a can-shaped or cylindrical topmark. At night, some of the most important show a green flashing light (Fig 14a).

Those on the starboard side of the channel are red, and either conical – known as **nun buoys** – or are fitted with a conical topmark. At night, they show a red flashing light (Fig 14b).

As well as these regular lateral marks, special **preferred channel marks** are often used to mark forks in channels, or the ends of shoals.

If the right fork is the major channel, it will be marked by a buoy very much like a port hand buoy, but with the addition of a horizontal red stripe.

If the left fork is the preferred channel, it will be marked by something like a starboard hand buoy, but with a red stripe.

**14.** When entering harbour in the USA, green can-shaped marks should be left to port . . . and red nun or conical marks to starboard.

| QUESTION | ANSWER |
|---|---|

Using the chart in Fig 7, but without using the clearing bearing on Gilkicker Point, plan the pilotage you would use to enter Portsmouth from the south west. Your destination is Camper and Nicholson's Marina, and for various reasons you do not want to go into water less than 2 metres below chart datum. There is a strong north easterly wind.

The words 'Boat Channel (see Note)' on the chart, refer to a local bye-law which requires you to keep to the boat channel on the western side of the entrance, shown on the chart by a black dotted line.

**ANSWER**

Spit Sand Fort NM 095°M

Leading line Memorial ø 054°M

When R can → 150yds, A/C 325°M

After 600yds, R can → close A/C 340°M thro' LHS of entrance

* Sandbanks → close 800yds inside entrance R can → 345°M 500yds to 'Ballast'

Marina

Pilotage notes are not intended to replace the chart, but to save you having to look up information on the spot. Some kind of shorthand is useful – you can invent your own, but in this example:

NM means not more than

ø means in transit with

R can means red can buoy

← means abeam to starboard

→ means abeam to port

LHS means left hand side

THE navigator of a slow boat can afford to be relatively relaxed about navigation. If things go wrong, they usually go wrong slowly, giving him time to think, and to adapt to the changing circumstances. Not so the fast boat navigator.

Navigating a powerboat is more like navigating an aircraft, combining a lack of space with a motion that makes it difficult to write (or sometimes even to read) and progress so rapid that fixes are obsolete before you've finished taking them.

Of course the fast boat navigator has one option that's not available in an aircraft – he can always slow down. But why not take a tip from our counterparts in the air, and overcome the problems by preparing for them in advance?

# 7
# A SENSE OF DIRECTION

## PREPARATION

The first essential is information.

**Charts** need to cover the right area, at a suitable scale, and be up to date. While it may be possible to make a complete passage on a single chart, a longer cruise may well call for a small scale chart of the whole area, several coastal charts at a scale of about 1:100,000; and a dozen large scale harbour plans.

Charts, like road maps, go out of date. But while it doesn't matter much if you find yourself on a motorway that wasn't there when the map was printed, running aground because you didn't know that the buoys had been moved is a different matter. All reputable chart publishers supply details of such changes, but if you don't want to correct your own charts, a reasonable second best is to avoid buying new charts until a month before you intend using them, and to update your entire chart folio at the start of each season.

You'll also need **tide tables** and **tidal stream atlases** – combined with other useful information in an almanac such as *Reed's* or *Macmillan's*. Unfortunately one year's almanac looks very much like the last: even professional skippers have been known to run aground by using last year's tide tables, so it's important to make sure you have the right one!

**Pilot books** and **sailing directions** are more a matter of individual taste. They take longer to produce than charts

and have a longer shelf life, so they are hardly ever bang up to date. But although it's as well to avoid using a pilot that's more than about ten years old, it's more important to have one that you feel happy with than the latest one to hit the chandler's shelves.

## PLANNING

There are no hard and fast rules about passage planning, and often far more 'right' answers than wrong ones. Essentially, it's a matter of

balancing your own inclination against the constraints which limit your freedom of action, then looking carefully at the details which will help or hinder you.

Imagine that you're in Perros Guirec, on the north coast of France. The chart is on the cockpit table, with a pilot book on one corner and an open bottle of Muscadet on the other, and the almanac is on the seat beside you.

The most obvious question is 'where shall we go tomorrow?'

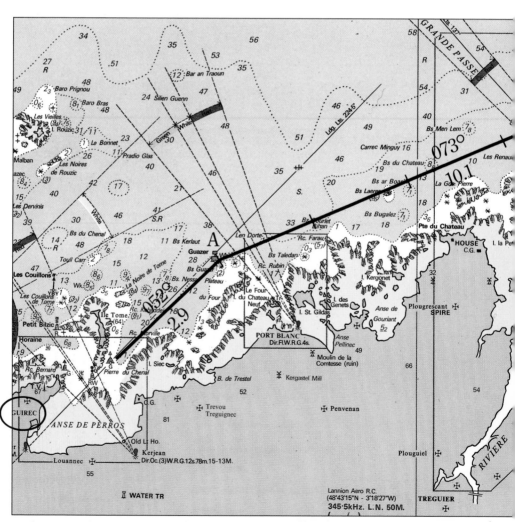

**1.** There are several interesting ports east of Perros, but we plump for Paimpol – easily reached at 20 knots.

The decision may be made for you: you might have to get back to the office on Monday, drop one of your crew at a ferry port, or meet up with friends. But let's assume that the consensus is that it would be nice to spend a couple of hours under way, and the rest of the day tracking down some *fruits de mer*.

Motor boaters tend to be eternal optimists about speed, but we'll be realistic and assume that we can maintain between 20 and 25 knots in open water. Allowing twenty minutes at each end for getting in and out, that limits the distance we can expect to travel to about 35 miles.

Looking eastward, the chart and pilot book offer several possibilities: Port Blanc, Treguier, Lezardrieux, the Ile de Brehat, or Paimpol. For one reason or another, we like the idea of Paimpol (Fig 1).

But the chart shows that, like Perros, its approach is not just shallow: it actually dries out. The **height of tide** will obviously be important, as will the opening times of the **locks** at each port (given in the almanac as well as in the pilot).

In this case, the Perros lock will be open from 0737 BST to 1037 BST, and the one at Paimpol between 0939 BST and 1239 BST. This drastically limits our freedom of action, but it all fits in quite neatly: even if we left Perros just before the lock shuts, we could still expect to reach Paimpol in time. Going the other way would have been a different matter!

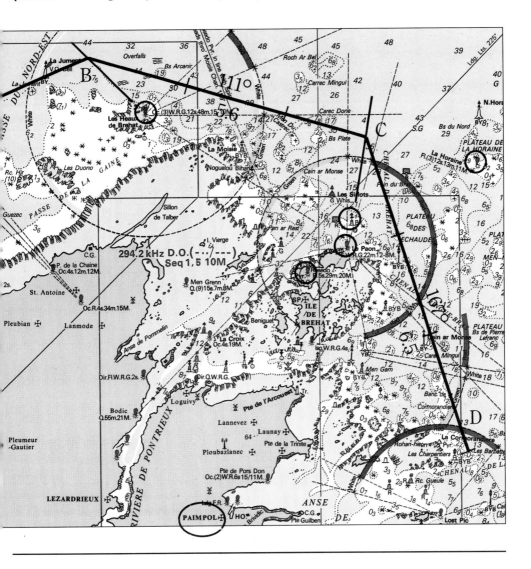

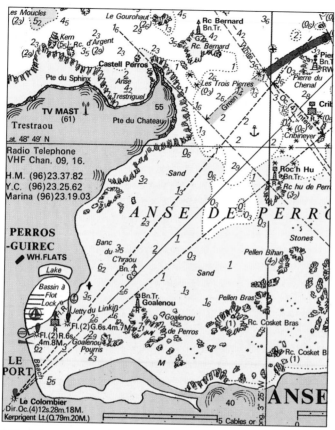

**2.** The lock opening time limits our scope, but the tide will cover most of the rocks in the Anse de Perros.

It also simplifies things. If we were to aim to leave at 0830 BST – that's half past nine local time, so there's time for coffee and croissants first – there will be about 8 metres of tide in the Anse de Perros (Fig 2). The same thing will apply to Paimpol (Fig 3), covering most of the rocks with a generous depth of water.

The next step is to decide on a route. As the most tricky bit looks likely to be the pilotage into Paimpol, there's something to be said for starting with that. Even here, there are several possibilities, but we'll pick the simplest, starting the pilotage at Les Charpentiers beacon tower (Figs 3 and 4).

For much the same reason, it makes sense to sort out the outward pilotage from Perros at this stage.

From here on, the job looks simple – just a matter of picking some convenient waypoints, and joining them up with intended tracks.

On this rock-strewn coast there are plenty of likely-looking buoys to serve as waypoints, but choosing them still calls for some care, because the scale of a coastal chart can be deceptive if you're fresh from looking at harbour plans. Two of those buoys are seven miles apart: 5° off course and another 5° of leeway would be enough to make you miss one altogether!

Besides, there are still the wind and tidal streams to consider.

The wind has two effects: it makes the sea rougher, slowing you down and making life generally less comfortable; and it causes leeway, upsetting your navigation and possibly pushing you towards hazards you thought you'd avoided. Both can be reduced, if not eliminated, with a simple rule:

● stay inshore if the wind is blowing you off, and stay offshore if the wind is blowing you on.

Tidal streams don't usually have much direct effect on the speed at which a planing boat covers the ground, although if a stream is setting across your intended track it's worth shaping a course to counteract it (Chapter 2). But they can make the sea rougher, especially off headlands or over uneven seabeds. Particularly rough patches, like the overfalls off Les Heaux de Brehat (Fig 5), are marked on the chart, so they can easily be avoided. In this case, however, we could go straight through, by adapting our timing so as to round Les Heaux at slack water at about 10 o'clock (BST).

In strongly tidal waters, it's worth aiming to make passages when the wind and tide are in the same direction. The sea is always flatter, so you'll probably save more fuel by not having to punch into it than you lose by having to fight the tide, besides enjoying a faster and more comfortable ride.

Then there's the 'what if?' factor. What if the oil pressure on one engine drops, ten miles out of Perros? There would be no chance of getting to Paimpol in time to catch the lock, and even getting back to Perros would be a bit nip and tuck.

L'Ost-Pic lighthouse, at the southern entrance to the Anse de Paimpol.

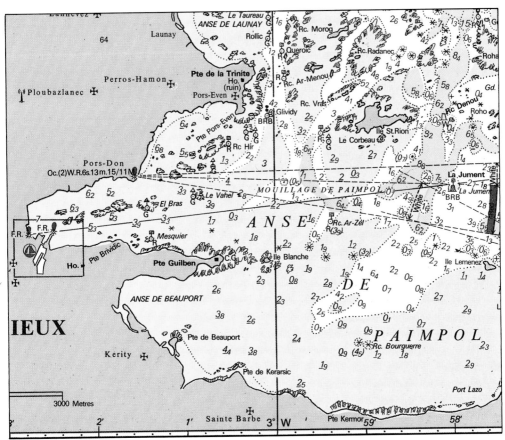

**3.** There will be plenty of tide at Paimpol, covering most of the dangers just as it did at Perros. But plan your pilotage before you leave.

PAIMPOL                     29 AUGUST

1009 BST        10·0M
1628 BST        1·2m

From Les Charpentier Bn Tr BYB
Steer 225°m for ½m (towards R Tr 1m)
A/c 270°m ½m R.can ◁
        270°m ½m R Tr La Jument ◁
If poss RW Pierhead hut ∅ RW lattice Tr 270°m
Otherwise 270°m 1m R Bn ◁ 300 m
        270°m 1m G Bn ▷ 200 m
        270°m 0·3m R Bn ◁ 200m G Bn ▷ 200m
        270°m towards pierhead (buoys)

Leave pierhead to port A/c 210°m to
lock.

**4.** The pilotage plan for Paimpol starts at Les Charpentiers, and includes tidal information as well as the bearings and distances between key landmarks.

**5.** The chart shows overfalls off Les Heaux de Brehat, so it's best either to round at slack water or avoid the area.

the pilotage involved in getting in might be so tricky that it would be tempting fate not to plan it in advance. And on a long passage, or in marginal weather conditions it might even be sensible to modify the intended route to keep within easy reach of suitable bolt-holes.

Having decided on the route, cast an eye over it once again, refining it if necessary to leave a suitable margin for error around hazards, and to make the most of any navigation aids such as buoys and lighthouses. Remember that the helmsman is likely to steer much more accurately if he's aiming for something than if he's staring at a swinging compass card!

Race-boat navigators often highlight the most important marks and hazards with coloured ink, but that's not

On a short coastal passage in fine weather you could argue that looking at ports of refuge is being unduly pessimistic. But on this passage, tightly constrained by the locks at each end, it's worth at least skimming through the pilot book to see what might be available.

The ideal port of refuge has

● unlimited access – no locks, swing bridges, or sand bars
● day or night entry
● simple pilotage
● good facilities – engineers, boat yards, doctors, etc.

Treguier and Lezardrieux fulfil all the requirements, but in other areas there might be no such places: you might have to allow for limited access, or such a good idea on a cruising boat whose charts may have to last more than one passage. A less drastic alternative is to highlight them with a pencilled circle.

Finally, measure all the courses and distances between waypoints and mark them on the chart, then transfer the whole lot onto a 'flight plan' (Fig 6).

## UNDER WAY

If the boat is pointing in the right direction at the right speed, it's almost bound to end up in more or less the right place at the right time.

So once the navigator has planned the passage, his most important job is to keep an eye on the log and compass.

But that only takes a couple of seconds: in between, there's plenty of time to look around, keeping a mental note of your position by relating

what you can see to what's on the chart, and seizing any opportunity that presents itself to grab a position line.

This is particularly important as you approach a waypoint, where the first job is to make sure that you really are in the right place.

**Never assume that what you can see is what you expected to see.**

Then check the course to steer to the next waypoint, allowing for wind and tide if necessary.

As you come round onto the new course, make sure that it

---

**6.** A flight plan summary of our complete passage is essential if we are to keep a check on our progress. This one is recorded in the Fernhurst *Motor Boat and Yachting Logbook.*

The chart should be marked up with tracks and waypoints, highlighting key features and showing distances to go.

looks right. The most common errors of all are simple ones: the navigator who skips a line in his passage plan, and asks for 095° instead of 075°, or the helmsman who misreads the compass and steers 200° instead of 020°!

Once you've settled on the

---

FROM: PERROS GUIREC    TO: PAIMPOL      DATE: 29 August

| | | | |
|---|---|---|---|
| HW Standard Port: 0932 10·6 | HW Standard Port: | | |
| LW Standard Port: 1601 1·9 | LW Standard Port: | | |
| HW Local: 0937 8·7 | HW Local: 1009 10·0 | | |
| LW Local: 1540 1·6 | LW Local: 1628 1·2 | | |
| WEATHER: SW 3 → NW 4 later fair mod/good | | | |

| | | Log miles | Eng hrs | Fuel |
|---|---|---|---|---|
| | | | P   S | P   S |
| Start | | 3792 | 205   204 | 3/4   3/4 |
| Finish | | | | |
| Day's run | | | | |

| TIME (ATD) | POSITION (LAST WAYPOINT) | LOG | TRACK | TIDE DIR | TIDE RATE | COURSE TO STEER | DIST TO RUN | SPEED | ETA | REMARKS | WEATHER | OIL | TEMP | CHARGE |
|---|---|---|---|---|---|---|---|---|---|---|---|---|---|---|
| | Pierre Jean Rouzic G. can | 052 | | | | | 2.9 | | | Aim to Lookout by 0900 BST | | | | |
| | A Gauzer R. can | 073 | E | 1.3 | | | 7.1 | | | | | | | |
| | Crublent R. Pillar | 073 | | | | | 2.3 | | | | | | | |
| | La Jument N. Card | 073 | | | | | 0.7 | | | | | | | |
| | B 1½m NW Les Heaux | 111 | | | | | 5.6 | | | Les Heaux ∮ Rosedo 140° 17 Steer towards La Horaine | SLACK WATER @ 1000 BST | | | |
| | C Chenal de Brehat | 167 | NW | 0.7 | | | 25 | | | BYTr ∮ Le Paon 195° M | | | | |
| | E. Card Pillar | 167 | | | | | 1.6 | | | →  | | | | |
| | N. Card Pillar | 167 | | | | | 2.4 | | | →  | | | | |
| | D¼ WNE Les Charpentiers | 225 | | | | | 0.5 | | | BYB BwTr Pilotage towards R BwTr | | | | |

Journey's end – the port de plaisance in the locked basin at Paimpol.

## PASSAGE PLANNING CHECK LIST

- ☐ **Steering compass,** swung and corrected for deviation
- ☐ **Log,** adjusted and/or calibrated
- ☐ **Echo sounder**
- ☐ **Plotting instrument,** e.g. Douglas protractor, parallel rules, or Breton plotter
- ☐ **Dividers**
- ☐ **Pencil,** 2B – a propelling pencil with spare leads saves having to carry a pencil sharpener as well
- ☐ **Rubber,** soft
- ☐ **Hand bearing compass**
- ☐ **Speed-Time-Distance calculator**
- ☐ **Clock or watch**
- ☐ **Charts,** appropriate area, scale, and up to date

- ☐ **Almanac,** especially for tidal data
- ☐ **Pilot**
- ☐ **Weather forecast,** wind and visibility
- ☐ **Destination,** approximate distance/time, facilities available
- ☐ **Fuel requirements,** aim to arrive with at least 20% of tank capacity in reserve
- ☐ **Ports of refuge,** access limitations
- ☐ **Tidal heights**
- ☐ **Tidal streams,** times of slack water through overfalls and wind and tide together
- ☐ **Any critical times,** e.g. to enter/leave harbour or round headlands
- ☐ **Time of sunrise/sunset**
- ☐ **Domestic,** e.g. need to visit a bank or supermarket
- ☐ **Hazards**
- ☐ **Key Landmarks,** especially to clear hazards
- ☐ **Route**
- ☐ **Waypoints**
- ☐ **Tracks and Distances**
- ☐ **Pilotage plans**

new course, you can tell whether you're likely to be able to maintain the same speed, and from that work out your ETA at the next waypoint.

### LOST

It's been said that a navigator is never lost – merely uncertain of his position. But I'd lay odds that most of us have been well and truly lost at least once.

Surprisingly few find themselves in serious trouble as a result: if anything, most groundings happen because the person in charge had convinced himself that he knew exactly where he was.

So take heart from the thought that admitting you're lost is half the battle.

Then the most important thing is to make sure that the boat is safe. Anchoring is one option, though it won't do much for your crew's confidence. Besides, in very deep water it's impossible, and in shallow water on a falling tide it may guarantee that you go aground instead of preventing it.

The alternative is to slow down, and to turn the boat onto what you believe to be a safe course. This may mean going back the way you came – allowing for the increased effect of wind and tide at low speeds – or altering course to go further offshore.

If you've been keeping a log book or flight plan up to date, you'll at least know where you were, and when. And you'll probably have at least a rough idea of the direction and speed you've moved since, so you can work out an approximately estimated position.

Then start thinking why it's gone wrong. Have we been steering consistently off to one side – and if so, which? Have I applied the variation or deviation the wrong way? Or allowed too much or too little for the effects of wind and tide? Have we been going faster than I thought? Or slower?

You probably won't come up with any definite answers, but you should at least end up with an EP on the chart and a strong suspicion that you are 'somewhere south of that'.

Having narrowed down the possibilities, you can start looking for clues.

Suppose, for example, that there's a church bearing 295°. Plotting that bearing on all the possible churches will, if nothing else, tell you where you are not. And if you can get two bearings they can be combined to give a whole crop of possible 'fixes' (Fig 7).

Checking with the echo sounder may well show that some of them are impossible, narrowing down the possibilities still further and giving you a much better idea of which courses are safe.

Then you can set off in search of more clues.

Try, if possible, to take bearings of the same objects again after you've gone far enough for their bearings to have changed significantly. If any of the new bearings marries up with an EP based on any of your first tentative 'fixes', you can be pretty confident that you'd picked the right landmark. And once you've positively identified something, you've got all the makings of a running fix.

None of this is easy: finding yourself is always much more difficult than not getting lost in the first place. To do it successfully, you need to be able to think clearly – and that means:

● Don't panic

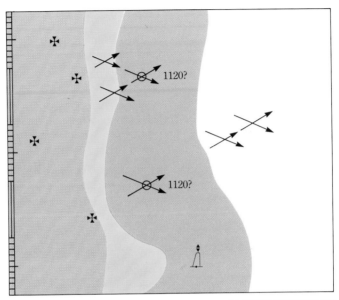

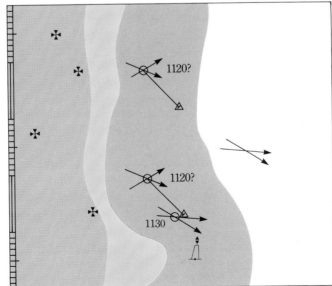

7. When unsure of your position, take bearings on unidentified landmarks to get several possible fixes. The echo sounder shows that some of them are impossible. Comparing subsequent bearings with EPs gives a positive identification.

- Hand over all the routine jobs (such as steering) to someone else
- Encourage your crew to tell you if they see anything that might help
- But avoid distractions – discourage them from asking questions until you've finished, turn the cassette player off, and keep the chart table tidy
- Be methodical – record every alteration of course and speed.

## LANDFALLS

Making a landfall after a long passage is always exciting. But it can also be uncomfortably akin to being lost. The coastline ahead probably isn't familiar, and your position is bound to be somewhat vague.

But while you don't have much choice about where to get lost, you can at least choose where to make a landfall.

The ideal would be a stretch of coastline with big, easily identified features, but with few deep bays, and no off-lying hazards. Unfortunately these three requirements usually seem to contradict each other: the most conspicuous landmarks are often either prominent headlands with deep bays in between; or islands surrounded by a generous

assortment of rocks!

But assuming reasonable visibility, crinkled, rock-strewn coastlines often give relatively straightforward landfalls because they are usually very well marked. Even if you have to start off with vague fixes based on very distant landmarks, they will usually be enough to let you venture close enough inshore to pick up the smaller marks.

More difficult are flat, featureless landscapes dotted with unidentifiable buildings. Faced with this kind of thing, the best advice is to aim for a point some distance off to one side of your destination so that you can be sure which way to turn when you reach land.

There is bound to be a nagging doubt about ploughing on towards the coast without knowing where you are. It's a Catch-22 situation, because the best way to get an accurate position is to go close enough to see plenty of landmarks. One solution is to use the echo sounder to follow a depth contour (Fig 8).

## FOG

There's no doubt that the navigator's worst enemy is fog.

Staying in deep water brings the risk of colliding with a ship or running out of fuel before the fog lifts, while going inshore increases the

chances of running aground. The tempting option of making for harbour may well combine the worst of both worlds.

The essence of fog navigation is careful steering and meticulous chart work – both of which are easier if you keep a constant speed. Inshore, the echo sounder can again be used to follow a contour line, perhaps leading you right up to a buoyed channel into harbour.

Most lighthouses and many important buoys have fog signals, so turning the engines off for a minute or two may let you hear a vital clue.

## NIGHT

Navigation at night is a different matter altogether: slow-boat navigators often prefer to make offshore passages at night and try to time their landfalls for dawn. That's because lighthouses and buoys all have individual identity signals which, in the case of major lighthouses, may be clearly visible and recognisable as much as fifteen miles away.

The main difficulty at night is the obvious one: unlit marks are effectively invisible. This in turn robs your surroundings of perspective, making it so difficult to judge distances that it's easy to mistake a lighthouse ten miles away for a buoy half a mile away. It makes it particularly important to check and double check the identification of every mark, and to allow a generous margin for error round hazards and headlands.

## DO I NEED TO NAVIGATE?

In this book we've put together a selection of navigational techniques – rather like a mechanic assembling a tool

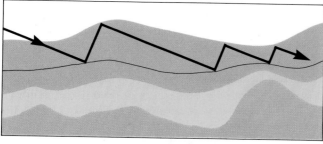

8. A depth contour can be followed by aiming to cross it at about 20°, then turning through 90° to get back into deep water.

kit. Like the tool kit, it includes some things that will only rarely see the light of day: running fixes, for instance, are certainly not something you're likely to use very often.

Others – working out tidal heights is a good example – should soon be so familiar that you'll hardly need to think about how to do them.

And just as a mechanic can do some jobs with just his bare hands, there will be times when you don't need to do any 'formal' navigating at all. This laid-back attitude is fine, so long as you can be sure
● of good visibility and daylight;
● of your own 'local knowledge' of the navigation marks and hazards;
● that there is enough deep water all around you to make your precise position irrelevant;
● and that the tidal streams will not be more than about 5% of your boat speed.

But why risk it? Not only is navigation all part of the fun of going boating, but – like the mechanic's tools – your navigation skills are more likely to go rusty if they're never used.

## LIGHT CHARACTERISTICS

Many navigation marks show lights, which can be distinguished from each other by their colour, rhythm, and period – all of which are shown on the chart in an abbreviated form: e.g. R means red, G means green, and W (or no colour specified) means white. The rhythm is a regularly repeating pattern made up of intervals of light and dark, and the period is the time it takes for one complete pattern.

| Fixed | F |
| Flashing | Fl |
| Group flashing | eg Fl(3) |
| | eg Fl(2 + 1) |
| Quick | Q |
| Group quick | eg Q(3) |
| Interrupted quick | IQ |
| Isophase | Iso |
| Occulting | Oc |
| Group occulting | eg Oc(2) |
| | eg Oc(2 + 3) |
| Alternating | eg Al WR |

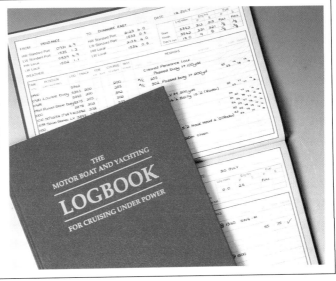

## MOTOR BOAT AND YACHTING LOGBOOK

The **Motor Boat and Yachting Logbook** featured in this book is tailored specially for all those who cruise under power with either twin or single engines. The log is designed for both traditional and flight-plan navigation and in addition to the standard log sheets includes a number of useful extra features.

The **Motor Boat and Yachting Logbook** is available from Fernhurst Books, 33 Grand Parade, Brighton, East Sussex BN2 2QA.

# MOTOR BOAT
## AND YACHTING

As the most experienced motor boating team in the United Kingdom, we deliver total coverage for cruising under power both in Britain and overseas.

Don't miss an issue this year – or you'll miss out on an exceptional package of features, boat and equipment reports and special supplements.

**PLUS** in-depth features on navigation, backed up by practical advice and expert evaluation – and we carry the largest selection of new and second-hand boats for sale.

To help you make the most of your boating, we're offering a special 20% DISCOUNT on a subscription to Motor Boat & Yachting – Britain's biggest selling motor cruising magazine.

Save time and money by subscribing today using the form below or phoning our 24-hour credit card hotline and receive Motor Boat & Yachting delivered to your door every month!

**BRITAIN'S BIGGEST SELLING MOTOR CRUISING MAGAZINE**

## SUBSCRIPTION ORDER FORM

Yes, I want to subscribe to *Motor Boat and Yachting* for one year at £_____. I enclose cheque (bank draft/international money order) to the value of £_____ payable to Motor Boat and Yachting. OR please debit my Visa/Access/Mastercharge/Eurocard/ American Express/Diners Club (delete as appropriate) for £_____

Please charge my credit card number

Expiry date of card_____

Signature _____

SPECIAL SUBSCRIPTION RATES – 20% DISCOUNT
UK £23.00; Europe £28.00; Outside Europe £36.00.
*Airmail rates on application.*

Name (block capitals please): _____

Address: _____

_____

_____

_____ Postcode _____

Please complete or copy this form and send it with remittance or credit card details to: Subscriptions Dept, Oakfield House, Perrymount Road, Haywards Heath, West Sussex RH16 3DH. Tel: 0444 445544. Or ring our 24-hour Credit Card Hotline on 0789 200289.

USA subscription enquiries:

Subscriptions Department, Reed Business Publishing Group, 205 East 42nd Street, New York, NY10017, USA.

Tel: 212 867 2080.

Company registered in England No: 53626

A photocopy of this form is acceptable.